Thoughts on Building Strong Towns

Volume 1

Charles L. Marohn, Jr.

DEDICATION

This book is dedicated to all of my friends and colleagues in CNU's NextGen; for inviting me in, making me feel welcome, encouraging me and for sharing so much of your knowledge and insights. I've benefitting in many untold ways from having such amazing people to connect with. I'm constantly inspired by you and humbled by your embrace of my work. Thank you.

Russ Preston, Eliza Harris, Ian Rasmussen, Scott Ford, Jim Kumon, Faith Kumon, Jed Selby, Tanya Pagalia, Peter Harmatuck, Mike Lydon, Edward Erfurt, Matt Lambert, Jen Hurley, Dan Bartman, Payton Chung, Will Dowdy, Andrew Burleson, Steve Mouzon, Jen Krouse, Joe Nickol, Karja Hansen, Ethan Kent and Atul Sharma.

CONTENTS

ACKNOWLEDGMENTS

My sincere gratitude to…
Justin Burslie, for always being the first edit as well as my pal,
Mike Kooiman, for giving my ideas life with his art,
Jon Commers and Nate Hood, for being my colleagues at Strong Towns,
Faith Kumon and Ryan Kelley of the Strong Towns Board,
My mentor, George Orning, and
Kirsti, for being the last edit and everything else that is important.

INTRODUCTION

Following World War II, the United States embarked on a great social and financial experiment that we know as suburbanization. It created tremendous growth, opportunity and prosperity for a generation of Americans that had just lived through economic depression and war. What we seemingly didn't stop to consider at the time was that the way we were building our places – spread out across the landscape – would be extremely expensive to sustain, far greater than the relative wealth the approach would generate.

While we financed the first life cycle of the suburban expansion with savings and investment, we financed the second by taking on debt. Entering into the third life cycle, our need to keep everything going became so desperate that we allowed our financing to become predatory. We're now at the end of this experiment, unable to prop it up or keep it going. We desperately need to find a different approach.

A study of the traditional development pattern – the way we built places for thousands of years prior to our current experiment – reveals many insights and much hidden wisdom that we have casually disregarded. This was knowledge our ancestors gained painfully through trial and error. There were few manuals, codes and standards, just an intrinsic knowledge across society on how to build great places. For them, it was *"how things were done."*

We seem to be at a pivot point in history, one that future historians will no doubt be able to analyze with crisp precision, clearly seeing where we went wrong and proscribing the solutions that will be obvious to them. For us today, living in the thick of transition, things aren't so clear. Like many, I'm trying to see through it. This is my contribution.

I've written for the Strong Towns Blog since 2009. My writing is an attempt to bring together insights from the engineering and planning professions with current events, trends and some historical context. While I do use a fair amount of statistics, my writing is generally not encumbered by numbers and charts. They tend to creep in where I feel credibility requires it. If you are not a numbers person, please don't let those rare instances bog you down.

What follows are my favorite essays from 2011. I've gone through and revised them all, providing more depth and additional background where I thought it would add value to the reader. I've tried to use links where there is significant source material and endnotes where I can provide more depth and needed references.

Keep doing what you can to build strong towns.

THE GROWTH PONZI SCHEME

In 2010, I had written a short piece that included a reference to the "Ponzi scheme" of suburban growth. It was a thought that emerged in the piece and, although I didn't go into great detail at the time, the term stuck. I began using it frequently, understanding that I would need to go back to the idea at some point and develop it further. After a reader asked me to do just that, I started what I thought would be a single essay.

The five part Growth Ponzi Scheme series is the widest read collection of essays I have ever written. On my blog, it was read by over 10,000 unique readers in the week it was published. I wrote a summary piece for the online publication Grist and it, too, was well received. The Business Insider ran a summary of it and reported over 100,000 views with a "double flame" to signify it was really hot stuff.

The following is the full series with only light editing. I've republished the summary article towards the end of this book.

Part 1. Trading near term cash for long term liabilities

The underpinnings of the current financial crisis lie in a living arrangement -- the American pattern of development -- that does not financially support itself. The great experiment of suburbanization that America embarked on following World War II has no precedent in human history. As it enters its third generation, the flawed assumptions that were overlooked are now coming back to bite us in a cruel way. Like any Ponzi scheme, there is only one way this ends.

In the great American experiment of suburbanization following World War II, we redirected our county's extensive resources into a living arrangement unseen at any point in human history. We abandoned thousands of years of history, knowledge and tradition in building cities and towns in order to try this new -- and completely untested -- approach.

In a way, this was an odd thing for such a pragmatic generation, having been conditioned on financial depression, scarcity and war, to undertake. I don't think they ever saw it that way, however. The Great Depression had cut short efforts to improve the industrial city. With the automobile offering the promise of mobility for all, it was seemingly within our grasp for each American family to one day live the life of European royalty, complete with a country estate outfitted with all the modern trappings. America's ascendancy and absolutely financial domination worldwide made this dream appear possible. We likely never stopped to think it through.

What is more puzzling -- at least to those that think about it -- is how there has been so little questioning of the logic behind this arrangement. American suburbanization is a grand experiment, but one where the hypothesis -- suburban development provides prosperity -- is never really tested. It is basically a law, not a theory, that has crept into our ethos. It is only the collapse of the housing market, along with the much less talked about but even more consequential collapse of the commercial real-estate market, that has allowed critics of suburbanization to migrate in slightly from the margins of the mainstream thought.

Suburban development has become equated with the American dream. Its continual propagation is nearly unquestioned. Even those who think we are in a deep financial hole that will take years to correct ultimately envision "recovery" to include a return to building more and more of this same pattern. But is that even possible?

Following World War II, four new ways of financing prosperity emerged from the lessons of the Great Depression. They were:

> ➤ Government Transfer Payments, where the state and federal governments made investments in local growth initiatives such as new roads, sewers, industrial parks and community facilities.

> ➤ Transportation Spending, particularly the interstate highway system and all of its local derivatives.

> ➤ Debt, which includes public sector debt but primarily is non-governmental debt including mortgages, commercial real estate loans, credit cards and more.

> ➤ The Growth Ponzi Scheme

Focusing initially on the first three, they all share two things in common. First, the initial cost to the local government for new growth is minimal. If the state or federal government provides a grant or low-interest loan to subsidize a project -- for example, the extension of a sewer or water line -- the local government may have to pay something, but it is nowhere near the total cost. Where the DOT comes in and builds a highway, widens a road, puts in a signal, builds an overpass, etc... there may be some local funds contributed, but again, the vast overwhelming majority of the money is spent by the DOT. When a developer comes into a community and uses leverage to finance a development project, and then when families or business owners come in and take on mortgages and real estate loans to acquire a property within the development, the local government spends little or nothing to make this happen.

That is the first characteristic these growth mechanisms share: a low initial cost of entry for cities. Even though the city gets local tax revenue from the new growth, it usually doesn't cost them much up front.

The second characteristic they share is that, with each increment of new growth, the city assumes the long-term liability of maintaining all improvements deemed "public". This typically includes sewer and water systems as well as roads and streets, but will also include treatment systems, pumps, water towers, meters and even storm water ponds. All of this stuff ages, degrades, breaks and ultimately needs to be replaced.

Put these two characteristics together and you have a key insight; **Cities routinely trade near-term cash advantages associated with new growth for long-term financial obligations associated with maintenance of infrastructure.**

To financially sustain itself then, a city or town utilizing the American suburban development pattern and making this tradeoff must believe one of the following two assumptions to be true:

(1) The amount of financial return generated by the new growth exceeds the long-term maintenance and replacement cost of infrastructure the public is now obligated to maintain, OR

(2) The city will always grow in ever-accelerating amounts so as to generate the cash flow necessary to cover long-term obligations.

Of course, with the suburban model, it is physically impossible for a city of finite dimension to grow indefinitely, let alone at amounts that accelerate forever. Even realtors are now starting to acknowledge that assumption #2 is not true.

Part 2. Case studies

In Part 1, I pointed out how cities routinely trade the near-term cash advantages of new growth for the long-term financial obligations associated with the maintenance of infrastructure. Cities pay little for new growth, but receive enhanced revenue from the development. In return, the city assumes the obligation -- and the long-term financial liability -- to maintain the now-public infrastructure.

At this point, it is easy for any of us to see the perverse incentives underlying this system. Politicians are generally inclined to worry more about the next year than an event that will occur a generation into the future. The public is likely to join them, discounting the future commitments they are making in favor of added financial benefit today. It is near-sighted, yes, but this type of thinking is also part of human nature.

It is tough to forgo real benefits today for the theoretical enjoyment of an uncertain future. The ubiquitous nature of dieting books, dieting plans, diet coaches and diet foods, all in a land of unprecedented obesity, does a great deal to validate this observation.

Examining the underlying finances of our cities at face value, one must acknowledge the following: In order for our development pattern to financially work, the amount of revenue generated by the new growth must ultimately cover the expenses incurred by the public for maintaining the new infrastructure. If cities are not raising enough revenue to repair and replace their infrastructure, the system cannot sustain itself.

Understanding this, I began to collect hard numbers from actual projects and compare those costs to the revenue generated by the underlying development pattern. This work continues, but in every instance I have studied so far, there is a tremendous gap in the long-term finances once the full life-cycle cost of the public obligations are factored in. Without a _dramatic_ shift of household and business resources from things like food, energy, transportation, health care, education, etc... and into infrastructure maintenance, American cities do not have even a fraction of the money necessary to maintain our basic infrastructure systems.

The following is a smattering of examples.[i]

Rural Road

A small, rural road is paved, with the costs of the surfacing project split evenly between the property owners and the city. We asked a simple question: Based on the taxes being paid by the property owners along this road, how long will it take the city to recoup its 50% contribution. The answer: 37 years. Of course, the road is only expected to last 20 to 25 years. Who pays the difference and when? Click here for this case study.

Suburban Road

A suburban road is in disrepair and needs to be resurfaced. The modest project involves repair of the existing paved surface and the installation of a new, bituminous surface. The total project cost was $354,000. I asked the question: based on the taxes being paid by the property owners along this road, how long will it take for the city to recoup the cost of this project.

The answer: 79 years, and only if the city adjusted upward its budget for capital improvements. For the city to recoup the cost of the repairs from the property owners in the development, an immediate property tax increase of 46% would be needed.

Street Serving High Value Homes

A group of high-value lake properties petition the city to take over their road. They agree to pay the entire cost to build the road -- a little more than $25,000 per lot -- in exchange for the city agreeing to assume the maintenance. As one city official said, "A free road!" I asked the question: how much is the repair cost estimated to be after one life cycle and how does that compare to the amount of revenue from these properties over that same period? The answer is that it will cost an estimated $154,000 to fix the road in 25 years, but the city will only collect $79,000 over that period for road repair. To make the numbers balance, an immediate 25% tax increase is necessary along with annual increases of 3% with all of the added revenue going for road maintenance.

Urban Street in Decline

An urban street section is in need of repair, which will consist of milling up and replacing the bituminous surface. The development along the street has stagnated for decades in favor of new growth on the periphery of town. As such, over the estimated life of the new street, the City expects to collect a total of $27/foot for road repairs. Depending on the alternative chosen, the cost for repairs is estimated to be between $80 and $100 per foot.

Rural Industrial Park

A rural town has an industrial park that is stagnating. The park consists of 25 rural lots sized at roughly 2 acres each. As part of an undertaking to encourage more development in the park, the city engineer recommended serving the park with municipal sewer and water utilities. While the city is pursuing a grant to pay the costs, everyone understands that they will assume the maintenance liability, so we asked the question: How much private-sector development is necessary to sustain the infrastructure. The answer: $316,000 per lot. This is more than double the current rate of investment seen in the park.

Suburban Industrial Park

A suburban industrial park with full utilities was constructed in 1995. Over the years, the park has filled out with a mix of commercial and industrial uses. City officials, pointing to the park as a major success, seek to double its size. I asked the question: If the city could spend the same amount of money today and have the same return in terms of private investment, would this be a good investment. To answer the question, we applied an inflation adjustment to bring the 1995 costs into today's dollars and then compared that against the current tax receipts. If a $2.1 million project immediately induced $6.6 million in private investment, and if all of the income to the city were devoted to paying off a bond to finance the improvements, it would take 29 years for the park to break even. In that time, the businesses in the park would rely on other taxpayers to plow the streets, provide police and fire protection, etc... Of course, the $6.6 million of private investment happened over 16 years and was often subsidized, factors that would extend that payback period significantly.

Small Town Wastewater System

A small town received support to build a sewer system from the federal government back in the 1960's as part of a community investment program. Additional support was given in the 1980's to rehabilitate the system. Today, the system needs complete replacement at a cost of $3.3 million. This is roughly $27,000 per family, which is also the city's median household income. Without massive public subsidy, this city cannot maintain their basic infrastructure. It is, essentially, a ward of the state.

Aggressive Expansion Project

A town that was represented in Washington by a major political powerbroker initiates a project that is designed to essentially double the tax base of the city. The project requires the dredging of a river to create a harbor, the extension of major infrastructure and the repair/replacement of existing utility systems. The projection is for the improvements to induce $32 million of private-sector investment. I asked the question: if the private-sector investment was guaranteed, how long it would take the city to pay off a bond for the project costs (since they are taking on the long-term maintenance obligation)? The answer: 71 years, far beyond the expected life of the improvements.

The last case is probably the clearest example of the perverse incentives of the American pattern of growth-based development. The city gets $9 million of federal money to induce new growth. It costs them relatively little. If the growth happens, they get the tax revenue. If it does not happen, they are out relatively little. This all works fine until the end of one life cycle, when large scale maintenance or replacement is needed. At that point, the costs vastly exceed the ability of the city to pay. Game over.

This is where the Ponzi scheme aspect kicks in, because what is the solution to this unsolvable problem? In America of the post-WW II era, that's easy: the solution is more growth.

When more growth is created, the city gets excess cash in the near term. That cash can then be applied to the old obligations. So long as the city continues to grow at ever-accelerating rates, the system works just fine. But like any Ponzi scheme, as soon as the rate of growth slows, it all goes bad very quickly.

If you want a simple explanation for why our economy is stalled and cannot be restarted, it is this: **Our places do not create wealth, they destroy wealth.** Our development pattern -- the American style of building our places -- is simply not productive enough to sustain itself. It creates modest short-term benefits and massive long-term costs. We're now sixty years into this experiment, basically through two complete life cycles. We've reached the "long-term" and we've run out of options for keeping this Ponzi scheme going.

Part 3. The Ponzi Scheme Revealed

So far I have examined how the American development pattern of the post-WW II era entices cities to exchange the near-term cash advantages of new growth for the long-term maintenance obligation of new infrastructure. This is a bad trade because the pattern of development costs more to maintain over the long run than it produces in revenue. In short, our development pattern is not productive enough to sustain itself.

A new development goes in. The developer builds the street and then turns it over to the city for maintenance. Houses are built and the city sees its property tax receipts rise. Imagine for a moment that the city took and saved the portion of those new receipts that was to be used for street maintenance. If the city did that every year throughout the life of the street, adding the new tax receipts to those already saved, and then used the cumulative savings to repair the street, here is how the cash flow diagram would look.

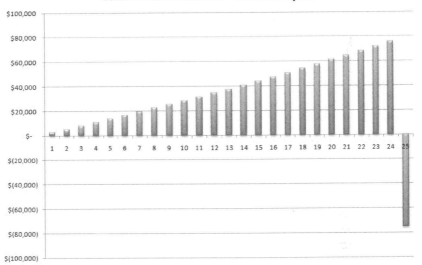

Everything looks great until the end of the street's life cycle, in this example, the 25th year. At that point, the cost of the repairs far outweighs the revenue collected. If the city were reduced to this one street, it would be insolvent.

But a city is not one street. A city has many Peters to rob in which to pay Paul. For example, if the project modeled above were repeated every other year -- a condition where the city was growing at a steady rate -- the cumulative cash flow diagram changes substantially at the end of that first life cycle. By adding the tax receipts from multiple projects together, here is what it would look like.

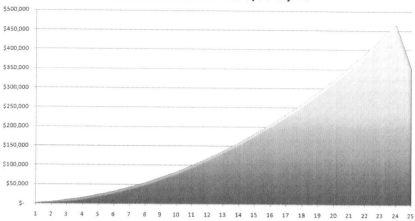

So growth "solves" the insolvency problem. As long as a city continues to grow, as long as it can continue to exchange near-term cash flow for long-term liabilities, it will be just fine. Or so it may appear at the end of the first life cycle.

Here is what happens during that second life cycle. The model I am using assumes that growth continues at the same moderate pace, with a new development of similar size added every other year.

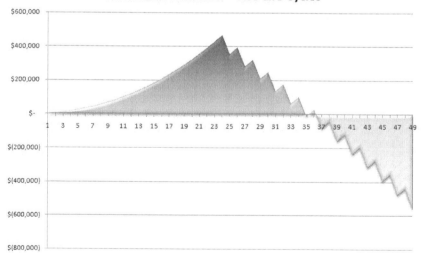

The results are obvious and devastating. When the private-sector investment does not yield enough tax revenue to maintain the underlying public infrastructure, the balance can be made up in the short term with new growth. Over the long run, however, insolvency is unavoidable.

We need to pause here and point out a couple of important things. First, this is actually a model of a well-run city, one that puts money away for future improvements. I've yet to see one that has such fiscal discipline. We can spend all day blaming politicians for wasting money on "big government" or giving unwarranted tax breaks to "the rich". These debates are ultimately tragic sideshows to the underlying lack of productivity in our development pattern.

Second, this model shows the impact of continuous and steady growth. In reality, that is not the pattern most cities experience. Most cities have a phase of rapid growth followed by stagnation and then decline, as described by Jane Jacobs in *The Economy of Cities*. Superimpose the financial underpinnings of the American model of development and the results are even more devastating - a flood of liabilities all coming due right at the time that growth is starting to wane.

Part 4. Going all in

The great American experiment in suburban development entices communities to take on long-term liabilities in exchange for near-term cash advantages, but as those liabilities cost the community more than the development creates in overall wealth, the approach ultimately results in insolvency. To forestall the day of reckoning, more growth is induced, setting up a Ponzi scheme scenario where revenue from new development is used to pay liabilities associated with old development. This is unsustainable, but that has not kept us from trying desperately to keep it all going.

Much of my thinking in this part was shaped by my reading of Richard Florida's *The Great Reset*, as well as follow-up research I have done into the causes of the Long Depression of the 1870's and the Great Depression of the 1930's.

While these events defy simple explanation, the Long Depression included an over-development of the nation's railroad system and corresponding malinvestments in speculative real estate associated with railroad expansion. Also, the increased access for farmers to broader markets helped create a commodity price crash, which was exacerbated by overproduction. Farmers with declining profits produced more to compensate, driving down prices. Price drops were so dramatic that some crops became more valuable for burning than eating.

The Long Depression persisted until there was, as Florida calls it, a "spatial fix". In essence, our capital and productive capacities were redirected from farm expansion and railroad-based speculation into industrialization and building of the industrial city. The result was the Second Industrial Revolution, a dramatically different living arrangement than the primarily agrarian America had known up to that point. For many people of that era, this was a painful transition.

Fast forward to the 1930's. Economists and social scientists argue over the causes of the Great Depression as well as the factors that ultimately ended it. What is clear is that the lack of fundamental growth in our real economy was made up for with an expansion in the paper economy. Industrialization had brought huge gains in productivity, production-capacity that actually outstripped our consumption-capacity. Leverage-driven speculation on continued profit gains created a financial bubble that, when deflated, proved destructive.

Years of New Deal spending failed to create enough demand to correct the imbalances. Spending for World War II provided a temporary recovery, but economists at the time were concerned that the end of war spending would send the United States back into depression. What happened next was another spatial fix; suburbanization. We redirected our capital and productive capacities to building suburban America and created the greatest economic advancement the world had ever seen. It was a very painful transition, especially for our major cities.

This is where I (humbly) depart from Richard Florida. It is not that I think he is wrong -- he argues that suburbanization has run its course and that the new, creative economy requires a spatial fix that will favor highly-connected mega-regions -- but that there is a pivot point critical to understanding our current situation.

That pivot point comes roughly one life cycle into the suburban development pattern, the time when the financial structure of the Growth Ponzi scheme starts to have outflows (maintenance costs) in addition to inflows (new growth on the periphery). This would have been roughly during the mid-1970's, when we were forced to leave the gold standard, had an energy crisis and experienced a convulsing economy characterized by the new term "stagflation". Another new term -- the Misery Index -- was used to measure the painful impacts of high inflation and high unemployment.

Once again, there is a ton of complexity here and I'm not trying to oversimplify things, but ours is an economy that relies on growth and, in the post-WW II era, growth has largely meant horizontal suburban-type growth with all of the related consumption. We embarked on a path that makes us reliant on new growth to generate excess wealth. When that new growth becomes old and starts to cost us money, it puts contraction pressure on the economy that counteracts the near-term, financial benefits of new growth.

The critical insight is to understand how we reacted to the end of the first life cycle of suburban development, when those maintenance costs started to come due and cut into our growth-generated wealth. This time there was no spatial shift as seen in the other large, economic corrections. Instead, we made a choice to double down on the suburban experiment by taking on debt.

We used debt to drive additional growth and sustain the unsustainable development pattern for a while longer. A lot of this debt was public debt, but we facilitated mechanisms for increases in private debt as well (for example, Fannie Mae and Freddie Mac early on and then subprime mortgages and securitization later). Here is a graph showing our public and private debt levels since the beginning of the suburban experiment. I have noted roughly the first and second life cycles of those initial investments.

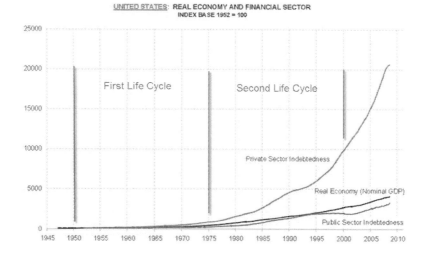

The first generation of suburbia we built on savings and investment, but we built the second -- and maintained the first -- using debt. Unprecedented levels of debt.

And in the process, we transformed our industrial economy into one based on consumption. As James Kunstler has noted quite often, when you take away the suburban-growth-related jobs from our economy, what you are left with is "heart surgery and KFC workers" (his way of saying highly-skilled professionals and low-skill wage earners).

This strategy is a disaster of monumental proportions for the United States. Not only have we created an entire economy based on a growth model that can't be sustained, in the process we have highly indebted our population. The quality employment opportunities available for the masses rely solely on the perpetuation of this unsustainable model, so we can't even work our way out of this mess. We've tied up our individual wealth into homes -- homes whose value is tied to community infrastructure that we cannot afford to maintain without continued hyper-growth, which we are now powerless to induce. So as our wealth disappears and our economy painfully grinds to a halt, we're left with no options to continue on this path.

And to top it all off, we've tethered our national psyche to the suburban ideal we call the "American Dream", our auto-based, utopia where everyone gets to live a faux version of European aristocracy on their own mini-estate.

Oh, and by the way, the American Dream, as so defined, is absolutely non-negotiable.

Our national economy is "all in" on the suburban experiment. We cannot sustain the trajectory we are on, but we've gone too far down the path to turn back. None of our dominant political ideologies can solve this problem. In fact, there is no solution.

Part 5. Rational Responses

There is a fine line one walks when doing a series like this, and I struggle with it myself. On one side of the line, there is a tremendous problem that has been identified, it has dramatic consequences that we are largely unaware of as a culture, and I want to yelp at the top of my lungs to make people aware. On the other side of the line is an awareness that the world does not want to listen to a sky-is-falling, doom-and-gloom, pessimist. We tend to call such people "crazy" and, in time, zone them out.

In this regard, I am certain that some people felt my last comment in the prior essay was unnecessarily provocative.

Our national economy is "all in" on the suburban experiment. We cannot sustain the trajectory we are on, but we've gone too far down the path to turn back. None of our dominant political ideologies can solve this problem. In fact, there is no solution.

I feel bad, but I am not trying to be provocative. There truly is no solution. This may be disappointing to those of you that have hung with this series because I have no magic bullet, no series of policies and no simple course correction that solves our current financial spiral. There truly is no solution.

Let me pass on an analogy I have used many times. Let's say that a person gets in a car accident. For whatever reason, they are seriously injured, maybe even disabled. They lose their job and, subsequently, their health insurance. Eventually they spend their savings, but they still have medical needs. Okay, what's the solution? There really isn't one, but there are ways for a person in this situation to respond that a third-party observer would call either "rational" or "irrational".

America is in a slow-motion car wreck. Lots of people are being hurt by it, some very badly. We've long lost our insurance by accumulating so much debt. We've also relinquished our production capacity. And we have little savings to speak of. What's the solution?

I wish I had one. I really do. I would be a very popular person, indeed. Unfortunately, all I can offer are rational and irrational responses.

For me, the rational response starts with this picture.

This is my hometown as it appeared in 1894. Today this street looks like Dresden in 1945, an empty wasteland of parking lots and low-value, partially-abandoned buildings. But in 1894, this place rocked. Look at it! Look at those buildings -- we'd give anything to have that back today.

Now ask yourself how this existed in the first place. How did we build such an amazing place before the home mortgage interest deduction? How did we accomplish this before zoning? Before the International Building Code? What created this place before we had state and federal subsidies of local water and sewer systems? Before HUD? Before DOT? Before the state highway system? Before Fannie and Freddie and subprime mortgages and collateralized debt obligations? How did we ever accomplish this before tax abatement, tax increment financing, SBA and local economic development?

Heck, we built this before the advent of the 30-year mortgage!

Here's the answer, and the key to the correction we need to make: **We built places that financially sustained themselves.** Do you know how I know this? Simple. If this place did not financially sustain itself, it would have gone away. In 1894, nothing was going to artificially prop it up.

This is not an anti-government argument. In fact, just the opposite. To pull off what my ancestors created -- a successful town in the center of the deep woods of Minnesota -- they had to have excellent government. Their future depended on it.

They had to organize themselves and use their collective resources very wisely. I look at the pictures of the beautiful way in which they maintained our now decrepit parks, the purposeful way in which they placed grand public buildings, the way in which they regulated the public realm and it is clearly evident to my trained eye that these people understood how to wring every penny of value they could out of their built environment. They knew the art and practice of placemaking.

Today we have largely relegated this art to Disneyland and isolated parts of the faux-downtowns we are trying to "revive". We have the New Urbanists to thank for resurrecting the lost knowledge of placemaking, much the same way engineers of the Renaissance recaptured the knowledge of the Roman bridges and aqueducts, an understanding literally lost for centuries. The transition in our understanding has been no less dramatic.

So there's the primary supporting strategy: **placemaking. We need to wring more value out of our places** and that is only going to happen if we understand how to create value in the first place. This is a monumental task because for two generations we have built our places without bothering to consider how they would be sustained (or whether they would even be worth sustaining). None of our public officials has ever asked the question: will this public project generate enough tax revenue to sustain its maintenance over multiple life cycles? Try asking that -- you will be amazed.

So a rational response is to start insisting that our places show a positive financial return. That will require a completely different approach to building our cities along with a completely different understanding of growth.

In addition to this, there are two irrational responses that we need to acknowledge. The first irrational response is to simply continue the present course until we are forced to change.

I'm astonished and more than a little depressed at the shallow nature of the public debate we are having over this crisis. Do we cut the budget or spend more? Do we raise taxes or reduce them? Does raising the debt ceiling signal fiscal responsibility or a lack of restraint? Do we build rail lines or highways? How do we restore housing values? How do we lower unemployment? And this is a sampling of the more intelligent lines of thought going on amidst the salacious and the ridiculous.

Nobody has acknowledged that a) the bubble economies of tech and housing were not financially real, b) we cannot "recover" to a condition that was not financially real in the first place, and therefore c) we need to start focusing on a transition to something close to reality, which is a long ways from where we currently are.

This brings me to the second irrational response; clinging to the belief that nothing needs to really change.

I had someone tell me, "*Chuck, I think you are right. I can't argue with a thing you say. But I believe in the ability of the American people to adapt and innovate and overcome any challenge we face.*"

Let me interpret this statement because I hear it all the time. "*Chuck, I think you are right, but I believe that someone, somewhere is going to come up with some trick or gadget that will solve this mess and keep me from having to change my lifestyle too much.*" I wonder if the Americans of 1870 or 1930 had this same belief.

I firmly believe that we have the ability to adapt, innovate and overcome. We will emerge from this a better people. But I don't see a way through this that allows us to keep the same lifestyle, the same living pattern and the same lack of productivity in our places. Like our innovative and resourceful ancestors before us, we'll find a way. But like those ancestors, it is going to involve a lot of painful change. Wishing for a miracle is fine, but depending on a miracle is irrational.

JUST ANOTHER PARK

(July 11, 2011) Today, public parks are seen as optional amenity to a community, something that you do in good times when you have the extra money or when you can get a donation or grant. In our pre-suburban development pattern, parks were looked at much differently. By working to understand the true nature of our original park layouts, we can reveal the character of our places and begin the process of unlocking the lost value stored in our traditional development pattern.

My twin home towns of Brainerd and Baxter, MN, are the perfect living experiments of the atrophy of an historic town (Brainerd) and the boom/bust cycle (Baxter), both inherent with the suburban pattern of development[ii].

In the summer of 2011, my colleague, Justin Burslie, and I grabbed a late night pizza after a meeting and decided to eat at Gregory Park. The park is one of my favorite places in Brainerd for some very complex reasons. While it embodies all of the decline and atrophy of the rest of the city, it holds a lot of hope and promise of renewal. I can stand in Gregory Park and hear the whispers of my ancestors, surrounded by reminders of what could be if we only understood what they were doing. I'm convinced that if we fixed Gregory Park, we could start slowing unwinding 50+ years of bad investments and neglect.

Now if you talk to anyone in Brainerd -- pretty much anyone inside or outside of the government -- they will probably agree that Gregory Park could use a little love. Some of the gardens need weeding, the grass could be better tended, the gazebo could use a little paint, the basketball court could use a new base, etc.... This is not the kind of neglect I am speaking of. What I am talking about is the complete misunderstanding of what Gregory Park is.

In its original design, Gregory Park was the focal point of the downtown of the city. It is the termination of Brainerd's original grand boulevard -- South 6th Street -- and the symmetrical axis on which the entire north side of the city is constructed. The intentional placement and design of Gregory Park was to reflect the value of this magnificent space through the downtown and all of the surrounding neighborhoods. You could stand anywhere along South 6th and see the park and, while standing on the axis of the park, have a framed view of Brainerd's prime boulevard.

It is this framed view that I am going to focus on today. What we have done to Gregory Park along this symmetrical axis reveals our suburban-era confusion over parks, how they reflect value back to the community and how to capture that value throughout the city.

The following picture is of an arch at the north end of the park. We took the photo facing south. This arch was installed in the 1930's, along with some other rock work, all symmetrical to the north/south axis. The arch itself frames the view. You can imagine my ancestors, who inhabited this space as what we would today call "pedestrians" (back then, they just called them "people"), walking through this arch on their way downtown.

After walking through the arch, the view should be of the central garden, the fountain and the boulevard into the downtown, with the city's (theoretically) magnificent and (again, theoretically) bustling commercial area visible in the background. Instead, you get the first hint that we have no understanding of this space. The view is blocked by this cheap-looking gazebo, which itself is completely random and out of place. Behind the gazebo you can see the alien spacecraft hovering in the sky at the top of the light pole.

Passing through the gazebo and the neglected (and poorly selected) shrubbery that surrounds the alien pedestal and "plaza" (the bricks of which have now settled and become misshapen), we should now be able to view the glorious downtown of Brainerd. But alas, we've given this park a nature band aid believing that the problem was a lack of trees. You can actually see how we messed up the vegetation on the sides a couple of decades ago too. Instead of copying the straight trunks and full tops lined up to frame the view from the right, we've selected different varieties on the left and placed them randomly. No symmetry. No views. And I'm sure there would be a protest if we removed these trees in the middle that are blocking the view, even if we did it to install a reflecting pool or some other appropriate feature.

Now we're past the Arbor Day rescue project and should be able to see the downtown only to discover that someone fell in love with street lights and decided to put some in the park. And a flag pole. Again, there is no symmetry to any of this. No sense of place or purpose. It is as if someone randomly went out and placed this light (which itself is out of place and makes no sense) and then someone else randomly came along and put down the flag pole with this tiny flag. I don't have a problem with the flag, but put it where the alien light is and then make it big enough to not be an afterthought.

Now we're finally through the park, having walked the entire axis, before we glimpse in any way what used to be the commercial heart of Central Minnesota. You can see the fountain here -- well placed -- and the 1930's rock work on the edges of the picture again trying to frame the view. You can also understand now why the "historic" water tower was placed where it was and, if you imagine South 6th lined with magnificent offices, shops, hotels and theaters as it once was, why the castle design for the water tower was not so silly. At the time it was built, it was all actually pretty cool.

Today that water tower is a white elephant, completely out of synch with the strip mall and parking lots it shades. People new to town gawk at it and think we're crazy to have built such a weird thing. If they only understood; we're not crazy, we have just lost touch with the essence of our town.

On second thought, maybe we have not lost touch with the essence of our town. After all, there really is no grand boulevard anymore. Long ago it was given over to the suburban-era obsession of moving cars at high speed. And there is no longer a downtown to frame. Again, in the suburban era, it was largely converted to space for storing our cars, the remaining businesses either torn down and replaced with drive-thru establishments or just plain neglected.

Maybe we've not lost the essence of our town. Maybe we're just trying to avoid looking at what it has become.

THE INFRASTRUCTURE CULT

Part 1. The ASCE Infrastructure Cult

(August 8, 2011) The American Society of Civil Engineers (ASCE) has just released a report that should be titled, *"Pretending it is 1952."* Like a broken record, ASCE is again painting a bleak picture of the future if American politicians -- as if they need to be plied -- won't open up the checkbook for our noble engineers. And in a way that the Soviet Central Committee would have expected from Pravda, the media and blogger world is sounding the alarm. This feels more like a cult than a serious discussion on America's future.

In the Long Depression of the 1870's, the railroads found they had over-invested in transportation capacity. Speculating on future growth and the returns on land development, they collectively built more rail lines than could be put to productive use. The result was a huge financial correction in which the private-sector railroads consolidated their routes, down-sized their unproductive infrastructure and put their reserve capacity into endeavors that had a higher rate of return. This was a painful, but necessary, correction.

The parallels to 2011 are obvious. We've built out the interstate highway system as it was originally envisioned[iii] -- although we opted to go through cities instead of around as planned -- and then we built even more. We poured money in highways, county roads and local streets. We have so

27

much transportation infrastructure -- a huge proportion of it with no productivity -- that every level of government is now choking on maintenance costs[iv].

While originally conceived in the name of "national defense," these investments were made in the service of "growth" and the belief that all increases in mobility, no matter how insignificant, would add to the overall prosperity. We've spent trillions to save seconds in the first and last mile of each trip, and what we've gotten is the fake prosperity of a land use pattern that is bankrupting us, housing bubble and all. This is the essence of the financial correction we are experiencing.

But there is one huge difference between today and 1873. Back then, while the railroads received government subsidies, they were still private businesses. They had to face financial reality. Today, our transportation systems are a public good funded through government spending. When the consensus of our political actors finds value in building more highways, the only reality check on the system is financial collapse.

We have a government that can borrow and tax as much money as needed and a Federal Reserve to print whatever Congress lacks the "courage" to raise. Combine that with a cult-like belief that the path to prosperity in America is to create more growth through more infrastructure spending, and you have a recipe for financial disaster. There is no negative feedback loop here that will slow this madness. Even Tea Party darling Michele Bachmann is a shill for massively unproductive transportation projects in her own district[v].

So in steps the American Society of Civil Engineers. If this is an infrastructure cult, they are the normal-looking guy that is there to reassure anyone who might think of leaving. That is probably what upsets me the most. I'm proud to be a civil engineer, but I will have nothing to do with ASCE and their self-serving, narrow view of the world. Consider the following from their report:

➢ ASCE estimated the "costs to households and businesses" from transportation deficiencies in 2010 to be $130 billion. (page 3)

➢ ASCE estimated the cumulative losses to businesses will be $430 billion by 2020. (page 5)

> ASCE estimated the cumulative losses to households will be $482 billion by 2020. (page 5)

If you add these together, the total cost to households and businesses is $1.042 trillion. Well, ASCE states that to reach "minimum tolerable conditions" (a pretty sad standard) would take an investment of $220 billion annually. Over 10 years, that's $2.2 trillion. Yeah, you read that right. The American Society of Civil Engineers wrote a report that suggested over the next decade we spend $2.2 trillion so that we can save $1.0 trillion. And we wonder why we're broke!

There are some things to understand about the $1 trillion as well. Those aren't losses to businesses and households as in money out of their pockets. This is the same old game I reported on extensively last year with the analysis of the benefit/cost analysis approach on the Staples overpass[vi]. The costs are all very real dollars that we spend. The benefits -- or in this case the losses -- are things like lost driving time and wear and tear on your car.

For example, say you work at a job making $25/hour. By ASCE math, I as an engineer spend untold sums and improve your commute by two and a half minutes in each direction. Each day that is five minutes saved. Each week it is 25 minutes. Each year I've saved you 22 hours. Over the 25 years of that road, I've saved you 540 hours which, at $25 per hour, is worth $13,500. Now, it is not just you that has enjoyed this tremendous windfall. Look around at the thousands of others on the road with you. Add them all up and, according to ASCE and the standard engineering approach, this transportation project is making us all very rich (even though the money never seems to accumulate in the average American's pocket, just leave it to pay for all of this).

ASCE is touting some other GDP costs as well, although it is hard to discern them clearly since, due to the ridiculousness of the numbers, they are forced to project out to 2040. Anytime someone has to project out that far to make an economic argument they are grasping. For some context, consider that 30 years ago inflation was over 10%, interest rates were over 15%, the Internet was still a decade and a half away, Ronald Regan was president and the big event of the year was the launching of the Space

Shuttle. Think they've factored in that kind of volatility? And you have to love the hubris of engineers making projections. What other profession would do a 30-year projection and come up with a precise number like $3.248 trillion?

ASCE estimated that, in a 30-year trend projection, we would have 400,000 more jobs in 2040 if we fully funded our transportation system (page 13 of their report). The ridiculousness of this number can't be overstated. NEW jobless claims **last week alone** were 400,000[vii]. We're supposed to make a multi-trillion dollar investment over the next three decades on a trend line projection that we'll have 400,000 more jobs? Are they serious?

One other thing in the report that made me shake my head was a table they had titled, "*Top 20 Countries and Economies Ranked by the Quality of Roads and Railroads.*" (page 17 of their report) For roads, the United States is ranked 19th behind such countries as France (2), Switzerland (3) and Germany (5), all countries that I have driven in. Anyone who has done likewise will attest that the standard highway in Europe is like a country road here in the U.S. I agree that their freeways are awesome, but they are also designed to connect towns, not feed strip development. I would attest that the "quality" in this case is less engineering-based and more a function of their adjacent land use not messing things up as ours does.

The table itself is based on an "*Executive Opinion Survey*" from *The Global Competitiveness Report for 2010-2011*. ASCE doesn't point out that, despite the sad opinion of our roads, the report ranks the United States as the fourth most competitive economy in the world. It is not really clear how we became so competitive with an infrastructure system ASCE ranked as a 'D'[viii] . Is it possible that there is more to an economy than infrastructure?

Don't misunderstand me; I want our infrastructure maintained. In fact, it's the common denominator of a Strong Town. But the reason why we can't maintain our infrastructure is not because we lack the money or are afraid to spend it. It is because the systems we have built and the decisions we've made on what is a good investment are based on the kind of ridiculous math you see reflected in this ASCE report. We spend a billion here and a billion there and we get nothing but a couple minutes shaved off of our commutes. All this simply means we can build more roads and live further away from where we work (or, as we call that here in America: growth).

Sixty years of unproductive infrastructure spending later, we are awash in maintenance liabilities with no money to pay for them. This is what happens when you have a government-subsidized, Ponzi-scheme growth system that, at all times, lives for the next transaction. America is all about new growth, which is why we don't even bother to question the findings in a study like this.

The ASCE report is an embarrassment to the engineering profession. The fact that politicians, journalists and bloggers[ix] are all lined up to mindlessly parrot these conclusions is pathetic. If we are actually going to get this country moving in a positive direction, we need a real understanding of how infrastructure spending is used to create value. We need a new approach to land use. We need to start building Strong Towns.

Part 2. ASCE "revises" report

(August 9, 2011) Yesterday I wrote about the ridiculous piece of propaganda issued by the American Society of Civil Engineers (ASCE) and dutifully circulated by the media. The report was designed to paint a negative picture of America's future if we did not pony up trillions for engineers to build and maintain infrastructure. The central argument was that continued decline of our infrastructure systems would cost us $1 trillion over the next decade. To avoid this calamity, according to ASCE, would cost us a mere $2.2 trillion. This is modern engineer-logic, where spending $2.2 trillion to save $1 trillion, is just plain common sense.

Interestingly, ASCE has now issued a statement clarifying its report. According to Brian T. Pallasch, CAE, Managing Director, Government Relations & Infrastructure Initiatives:

> *"ASCE is revising figures reported in the release of its recent study on the economic impact of underinvestment in transportation infrastructure. The original report dramatically underreported the negative effect of Americans' personal income due to failing transportation infrastructure. The report shows a clear and rapidly-expanding negative impact on Americans' pocketbooks in both the near and long term, and a dramatically accelerating negative effect on GDP in the near- and long-term. Our original release projected that Americans' personal income would drop by $930 billion by 2020 but recover slightly in 2040. The data clearly show that the effects will be dramatically more negative, with $3.1 trillion in personal income losses*

by 2040. The negative effects on American GDP will also expand dramatically over time, with a near-term loss of $897 billion and a near-tripling of that loss to $2.6 trillion by 2040."

Ostensibly they want to be taken seriously.

Let's focus on the revised GDP number of $2.6 trillion by 2040. In the past, I have written about how the Federal government is using overly-optimistic projections of GDP growth and how just slight changes downward in those projections would mean trillions in lost GDP (see the essay "Downgraded" included in this book). In fact, a minor drop in the growth rate from 4% to 3% would cut $2 trillion out of the GDP by 2020.

Sometimes when you are throwing around a trillion here and a trillion there, it all gets kind of lost in translation. To provide some clarification, I started with the 2010 GDP of $14.7 trillion and projected out three different growth rates through 2040, ASCE's study window. I then compared that to ASCE's projection for cumulative lost GDP. When you bring these projections out to 2040, here is what it looks like:

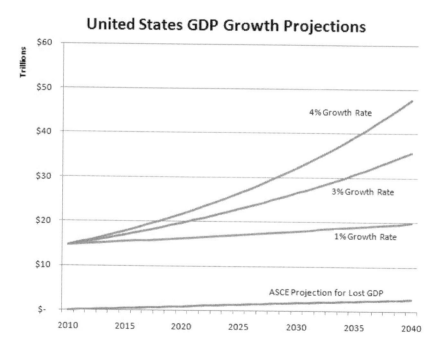

This illuminates the absurdity. Even in the scariest scenario envisioned by

ASCE's report, GDP loss amounts to a fraction of the *estimation error* between the different assumed rates of growth. When you get to 2040, the $2.6 trillion in cumulative loss pales in comparison to missing the overall growth rate in the projection by just 1%. This is statistic silliness.

This also shows how ridiculous 30-year projections are. Do we really have a clue as to what our economy is going to look like in 30 years? The hubris involved in making a projection like this, with the precision they offer, is laughable.

Just for the mental exercise, let's take ASCE at their word and assume we lose $2.6 trillion cumulatively in GDP. Assuming the federal government captures roughly 20% of GDP through taxation[x], a $2.6 trillion loss in GDP would mean the U.S. Treasury would lose out on $540 billion in revenue over the next 30 years. Contrast that with the $6.6 trillion they are suggesting we spend over that same period and you start to get a sense for how backward this logic is.

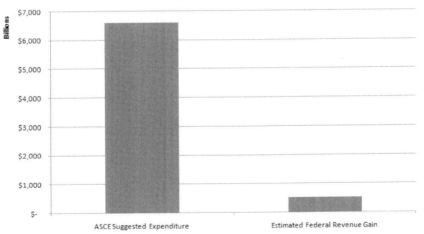

Federal Costs and Revenue Gain from ASCE Recommended Transportation Spending (30 years)

When I said yesterday that this felt like a cult, this is what I meant. We have collectively believed for so long that spending on infrastructure is the key to prosperity that we don't even bother to check and see if it is. I don't think ASCE even checked their numbers. They simply looked at the estimates for lost GDP and said, *"That sounds pretty bad."* Then they looked at their projection for how much money they and their allies wanted to shoot for in the appropriation and said, "*That sounds right.*"

They are all so brazen they didn't even bother to notice that the amount they wanted to see spent was more than the amount they claimed we would lose.

Or did they notice but thought we would be too stupid to figure it out? If they did, it worked. I've searched all over Google news and can't find a single story or blog that did anything but parrot this report's findings. Just like in a cult, nobody questions the story they are told.

You'll note ASCE never took the annual transportation appropriation they were calling for and ran that dollar amount out to 2040. That would not have been good propaganda.

ASCE's report is an embarrassment to the engineering profession. This revision merely adds insult to injury.

Part 3. ASCE claims we made "misstatements"

(August 25, 2011) The Seattle Times recently featured a column written by Kathy J. Caldwell, president elect for ASCE, responding to a Neal Peirce column that first appeared in the Washington Post[xi] but was likely syndicated in Seattle as well. Caldwell indicates that we at Strong Towns made "misstatements" in that we got the "purpose of the study wrong". Here is what she wrote:

> "*Neal Peirce chose to trumpet the misstatements made in the "Strong Towns' blog about American Society of Civil Engineer's "failure to act" report instead of looking into the report's intent himself ["Prioritizing the nation's infrastructure investments,' Seattletimes.com, Aug. 20].*
>
> *If he had, it would have been clear that the study's purpose was to show the expected negative effects of America's current level of investment in surface-transportation systems, not prescribe ways for infrastructure dollars to be spent.*"

My critique of the ASCE report was that it was a ridiculous piece of propaganda that (1) intentionally distorted the numbers by projecting the "*negative effects*" cumulatively over 30 years and the needed "*investments*" in single year increments, and by doing so it (2) actually didn't recognize the fact that the *"investments"* had a far greater cost than the *"negative effects"* and thus (3) failed to provide any relevant information to decision-makers and policy advocates.

My critique was also of the politicians, media and bloggers who blindly parroted the ASCE narrative in a call for more spending.

While it is true that the ASCE report does not, as Caldwell indicated, *"prescribe ways for infrastructure dollars to be spent"* (it does not recommend specific projects or appropriation methods), it pretty clearly follows the bad-things-will-happen-unless-we-spend-more-money approach.

The press release from ASCE and the report speak for themselves. In fact, here are the headings from the different sections of the press release. Read these and ask yourself if ASCE is playing the role of truth-seeker or propagandist.

- American businesses and workers will suffer

- Families will have a lower standard of living

- Modest investment needed

In fact, just read the heading of their press release:

> *"American Society of Civil Engineers releases first-ever report on how U.S. economy and family budgets will fare if America fails to fund surface transportation improvements."*

Caldwell and ASCE are insulting us even further if they are going to try and say now that their intent was solely to point out the problem but they had no suggestion as to what the policy response should be. Clearly, the response for a country that *"fails to fund"* is to fund, is it not? What are they trying to suggest by saying that only *"modest investments"* are needed to forestall *"suffering"* and a *"lower standard of living"*? Why mention the *"modest investments"* at all if their only intention was to point out the problem?

The reality is that I've been pointing out this same problem for years: the United States has more infrastructure than we have the money to maintain.

And as ASCE's report so vividly demonstrates, the public's return-on-investment for this system is horrendous. What we have built is simply not productive enough -- it does not generate enough prosperity that can be captured through taxation -- to sustain itself.

Where we break from the propaganda machine at ASCE is in pointing out that "*modest investments*" are needed to keep this Ponzi scheme going. Overlooking the fact that the cost of the so-called "*modest investments*" exceed the cost of the estimated "*suffering*", I'm not calling for "*modest investments*", implied or otherwise. I want an entirely different approach.

In fact, Kathy J. Caldwell provides a perfect analogy for a different approach in a statement she makes on her website. In response to a question about ASCE's focus for the year ahead, she writes:

> *"Many of our members are suffering from the impacts of the current recession, which impacts ASCE as an organization. Consequently, our members rightfully expect ASCE to make similar tough financial, operating, and management decisions. We must systematically review every element of the Society, going beyond the work of the Program Committee, which looks at only 10% of our overall budget. A benefit-versus-cost analysis must be performed to identify areas of the Society that are underperforming or unproductive and, therefore, should be corrected or suspended. We need to trim the trees and weed the garden, without destroying the landscape."*

To get America back on the right path, Caldwell and ASCE should simply apply her organizational philosophy to the conclusions contained in the next ASCE report instead of promoting -- implied or otherwise -- a mindless continuation of the status quo.

MEASURING PRODUCTIVITY

(August 15, 2011) In an age of austerity, we need to make our public investments go further. No longer is it acceptable to simply analyze public projects in one dimension, such as cash flow or job creation. Our projects need to leverage our limited revenue to do all that and much, much more. Our top priority today needs to be on making our places more productive.

Those of you that have followed my work on the Strong Towns blog or podcast, or attended a Curbside Chat[xii], have seen me refer to the work of Joe Minicozzi[xiii]. While the Strong Towns approach often starts with the public cost for infrastructure and then compares that to the revenue yield from the property it serves, Minicozzi comes at the productivity equation from a different -- and thought provoking -- angle.

Let me share an analogy from Minicozzi: When we look at the productivity of a car, we measure it in miles per gallon. The question we ask is: how many miles does a car travel per gallon of gas used? We are comfortable with this approach because it is vastly more logical than a miles per tank calculation. Nobody asks: how many miles can I travel on one tank of gas? We all understand that, while a Hummer may have a bigger gas tank than a Honda Civic, it does not make nearly as productive use of gasoline.

Cities often vigorously pursue that large business -- think Wal-Mart -- instead of the small ma-and-pa shop under the guise that the large business is going to generate more tax base. The same with the big house in the suburban subdivision. That sheetrock palace is paying a lot more tax than the little house on the city block. Isn't it logical that a city will be better off if they have more of these large businesses and homes?

Minicozzi's analogy would suggest that revenue per lot is a poor measure of success. The large business may provide a lot of tax base, but it also chews up a lot of land and requires a lot of infrastructure. Same with the house on the large lot. A better way to measure success, and true productivity, would be to look at the tax base on a per acre basis.

Seem abstract? Let me give you a real example.

I have done a lot of work with the City of Pequot Lakes, MN. Currently I am working to expand their Grow Zone, an area in town where we helped establish a form-based code two years ago as part of a plan to promote business development. Last month we analyzed two streets that had just been reconstructed as part of a routine city maintenance project. What we found affirms Minicozzi's premise.

The street reconstruction cost $180 per foot. These costs were actual construction costs from 2010 so there is nothing theoretical about them. The tax base calculations were based on (1) the city's current budget, (2) the city's current tax rates and (3) the actual assessed value for each property. I assumed a 20-year life span for the street and put the total revenues collected over that period of time into a present value (at 4% for anyone interested). The results reveal two streets in the heart of the city's downtown that are not even close to being productive.

Street #1

Total cost for street reconstruction: $104,400

Total revenue collected for maintenance over one life cycle: $23,400

Revenue gap in current configuration: ($81,000)

Percent of project covered by adjacent tax base: 22%

Street #2

Total cost for street reconstruction: $126,000

Total revenue collected for maintenance over one life cycle: $50,000

Revenue gap in current configuration: ($76,000)

Percent of project covered by adjacent tax base: 40%

These are streets -- especially Street #2 -- that, if you asked a local to name the five most productive streets in town, would assuredly be on the list. It has some of the largest businesses and the town's major employers. Even so, the taxes collected from the adjacent properties are not even remotely close to covering the basic maintenance costs of the streets that serve them.

The premise of our work there is not just identifying this imbalance, but solving it. The standard "miles per tank" approach would suggest that we seek to attract another large business to locate along this street. That would be the wrong move.

In the spirit of Minicozzi's work, we analyzed the yield from each property along the streets. The one with the highest total value is also one of the city's largest employer and a business that the community values greatly. It consumes five acres in the heart of downtown and, while it pays over $14,000 per year in property tax to the city, the yield is only $2,860/acre.

In contrast, a small little shop that had lost its tenant and was currently sitting vacant -- a place that, quite frankly, nobody in the city government or local business communities much values -- paid only $1,200 per year in property tax. However, it only consumed a quarter of an acre. Its yield: $4,960/ acre.

To be successful, the City of Pequot Lakes does not need to attract another large employer to build a new mega-business. All it needs to do is get this run down little shop reactivated -- something that is actually much easier to do -- and then create an environment that would allow 20 more of them to be built along this same street. These are small investments within the grasp of local entrepreneurs, very doable over a longer time horizon. When all you need are a bunch of these modest-sized establishments, all of a sudden there is tons of room for growth.

I can already hear the chorus of objections from the "jobs first" crowd. They will say that the low-yielding, big business is creating a lot of jobs -- many of them high-paying -- and this little shop, even on a good day, will create few. They will argue that economic development is all about job creation and so focusing on this small end of the spectrum is missing the point.

I could question the basis of that assumption, but for brevity's sake let me instead point out the obvious fact that always makes these economic development people angry. From the city's perspective, there could be a thousand jobs at that business and a billion dollars in sales run through there. None of that will change the property value and thus none of it has any bearing on this city's revenue, which comes from property tax and not sales or income taxes. You can argue that tax laws should be changed to provide for a local income tax and a local sales tax (some places have one or both of these, but not Pequot Lakes), but until that happens, the only way this street pays for itself is by becoming more productive from a property tax standpoint.

That is not to say that jobs are not important. They are. But they are one factor in many. We can spend a million dollars to attract or create a job, but if that job doesn't generate any financial return to the community, it is going to be hard to repeat that effort. Viable, long-term jobs will emerge from a productive land use pattern, not in spite of one. In an age of austerity, we need to think in multiple dimensions and make our public investments go further.

This brings me to a final, obvious question: If these streets are not productive, why are we building them this way? There is a long answer to that, but the short version is this: we've not had to bother about productivity until now. Since the end of World War II, we've been so wealthy and had so much growth that, for most parts of the country, the productivity of our places did not matter much. If it created a job, it was good. If it brought in a new business, it was good. We didn't ever pause to worry about what happens when the maintenance bills come due.

Those bills are due now, and more are arriving each day. We don't have anywhere near the money to maintain so many unproductive places. What we face is a choice between a chaotic reset or a strategic contraction -- one where we intentionally divert our limited resources into those endeavors that are most productive while we seek -- block by block and neighborhood by neighborhood -- to improve the productivity of our places.

I'm optimistic, at least, that we still have time to choose.

WE DON'T NEED NO TRANSPORTATION

(February 7, 2011) Door to door transportation for K-12 students may seem to be a compassionate policy from a society that values both students and education. That may be the intent, but the transportation mandate ultimately takes money from classrooms to subsidize our inefficient, post-WW II development pattern. In the end, it also devalues traditional, neighborhood schools in favor of the remote, campus-style we now build. A Strong Towns approach would be dramatically different.

We were heading into town for swimming lessons one Saturday when I drove by one of the old elementary schools I went to as a kid. Its name -- Lincoln Elementary -- tells you that it is old. Back in the day we used to name schools after people we admired. Today we name them in cheerful commemoration of the places we had to destroy during their construction. For instance, the newest school in my district is called Forestview, which was built in the clear cut forest across from my old family farm (took out a couple of my old tree forts in the process). In the neighboring school district they have Eagle View Elementary. The only eagles you will see there were built by the Chrysler motor company in the 1990's.

There arc many other differences that are more significant, but for today I want to focus on transportation. Busing is something that the students that used to attend Lincoln school did not need but which the children of Forestview must have.

Understand that my parents still live on the old farm and so they are living in the house closest to Forestview. Since they literally could not walk there safely on a school day – the area is just not configured to make it happen -- it is fair to say that few children could. That is not to suggest that Lincoln Elementary is safe. It is not. The street outside the front door -- literally feet from the door - was made into a highway. It is a chicken or egg argument as to whether the drop in enrollment at Lincoln was the cause of or a product of the neighborhood becoming inhospitable for families. Either way, Lincoln Elementary is now closed, a large portion of the playground turned into a parking lot (a higher use, by local standards).

So like most districts across the country, especially those in small towns or suburban areas, students arrive at their local school by bus or by car. A few will walk. In fact, my school district's policy is to only pick up those students that live further than a mile from their school. This was increased from a half mile a couple of years ago as a cost-cutting measure. The glaring inequalities and perverse incentives of this system are obvious[xiv].

Like nearly every American school district, ours is struggling with how to do more with less. And not just more, but much, much more. And not just less, but much, much less. Improving the educational performance of our youth in an age of austerity may be our generation's defining challenge.

So here's an idea I'll toss out from the Strong Towns mindset: How about we rethink our approach to busing?

Again, I'm not trying to get into a broader discussion on race. I'm not thinking that big. If you want to knock me down for my ignorance, please do. But hear me out first.

The State of Minnesota -- and I suspect this holds for most, if not all, states - requires school districts to provide transportation to all students in their district[xv]. The districts are given money for this undertaking. The mandate is fairly loose - at least loose enough where districts can exempt some kids that live close and charge fees for kids involved in activities that ride alternative schedules. Nonetheless, if a child wants to ride the bus, the school has to pick them up and drop them off.

As school budgets have been squeezed, districts have found creative ways to shift funding from transportation into the classroom. Such tactics have drawn the ire of some including those at MN2020, who have written a report calling for the establishment of a separate fund for transportation that could not be shifted to other causes.

From the MN2020 website:

> *"Our latest report, Wrong Way: Minnesota's School Transportation Funding Disparities, explores how disinvestment forces district administrators statewide to either siphon funds from transportation to pay for basic needs or shift classroom dollars to cover getting students to and from school.*
>
> *District leaders make budget-balancing decisions that include adopting four-day school weeks, cutting routes which lengthens time spent on buses, adding a fee or outright eliminating transportation for after school activities and increasing the distance from school that the district offers busing."*

Respectfully, what if MN2020 has it wrong? What if we went the other way and shifted all transportation funding into the classroom? We if we ended the mandate for schools to provide transportation?

If you look at the MN2020 report, districts that have neighborhood schools in higher density, walkable areas actually have a surplus in transportation spending they can use for other needs. In contrast, large rural districts and suburban/exurban districts run huge deficits, taking money from the classroom to fund transportation.

Let's ask a pointed question: How many of the students in those rural, suburban and exurban districts live and work on farms? In other words, what percentage of their parents must be located in a remote area for their livelihood?

I don't know the answer, but my experience here in Minnesota tells me it is a very small percentage. I'd guess less than 3%. This means the remainder live far from school due to personal preference. In the free market, they have selected a remote location that requires school districts, mandated to provide transportation, to take money from classrooms to pick up and drop off their kids.

This is an important observation. By mandating that school districts provide free transport to all kids, regardless of any other circumstance, we have created a situation where parents do not have any incentive to consider the true cost of busing their children when they decide where to live. They can live two blocks from school or twenty miles from school, the cost to them is the same: nothing.

What if we asked those non-farm parents to pick up the tab? What if that money could be redirected to the classroom? Using my local school district as an example, the numbers could be huge.

My school district was scheduled to spend $3.4 million in transportation costs for the 2011/2012 school year[xvi]. That seems in line with the costs reported in the MN2020 report. With a starting teacher in the district making roughly $41,000 in salary and benefits[xvii], we could add over 80 new teachers right now if we stopped subsidizing transportation. That would be a 20% increase in staffing, potentially a game-changing amount.

Here's my proposal: What if we abolished the mandate that schools provide transportation to all students, but required them to still provide it to children that lived on farms (or whose families had careers that required them to live in a remote location)? For all other children, transportation would be provided as a fee-for-service offering. We then subsidize children from poor families (many of whom live close to the old schools anyway).

Besides the fact that it is nearly politically impossible to get people to pay for something they have been receiving for free, what are the objections?

It makes no sense that we continue to abandon neighborhood schools in favor of these remote campuses that require every child to be bused to. The only reason this continues to happen is that we've made transportation a sunk cost -- money a district has to spend regardless -- and so the cheapest way to do it is to make it large-scale. In the meantime, the transportation mandate is simply another perverse incentive for people to make lifestyle choices that ultimately have huge, financial costs to society.

The current calculus is going to change dramatically when gas goes to $4 per gallon and higher. When that happens, you'll hear school administrators and lawmakers howl that we are forcing all of these financial burdens onto the schools, robbing the classrooms of funds, and that they need ever-more money to provide ever-declining service.

Here's the money. We just need the will to actually make this policy change.

MISUNDERSTANDING MOBILITY

Mobility's Diminishing Returns

(April 4, 2011) We like to believe that the United States is the land of opportunity. We also believe, for logical reasons, that increasing mobility increases opportunity. But does this correlation always hold true? When do we go too far, to the point where the cost of improving and maintaining mobility actually stifles opportunity?

For those of who demand a rigorous statistical analysis for each idea put forward, stop reading right now. I am not going to help you here and, while I appreciate your passion, I'm not going to be able to answer all of your emails either. This essay challenges decades of facts, figures and statistics so, in a room full of empiricists, I would be shouted down vigorously. It should be noted, however, in the tradition of Albert Einstein, amongst others, that it frequently is not the answer but the question that poses the deepest insight.

Today I ask the question: Have we overvalued mobility?

Randall O'Toole, whom I've had friendly debates with in the past, is a champion of both the auto-based transportation system and mobility in general. His argument is essentially that there is a correlation between mobility and prosperity, that the more mobile a society is, the more at liberty people are to follow endeavors that enhance life, liberty and the pursuit of happiness. Greater mobility increases job opportunities, shopping selection, service competitiveness, school choices and even the gene pool people have a chance to select from when seeking a mate. There is no question that, in a broad sense, he is correct.

The first chapter in his book, *Gridlock: Why we're stuck in traffic and what to do about it*, is called *"Land of Mobility"* and in it he makes the case that increasing mobility increases prosperity. Specifically he says:

> *"Economists estimate that construction of new highways contributed to nearly one-third of the rapid economic growth the United States enjoyed in the 1950's and a quarter of the growth in the 1960's. The growth wasn't generated by construction jobs; it came from the increased mobility offered by new roads. It may be no coincidence that our economic growth slowed as highway construction tapered off in the 1970's and 1980's."*

(I'll note that the slowing of economic growth also correlates to the end of the first life cycle of the new roads. This is the time that the long-term cost of maintenance started to kick in.)

Let's examine mobility in a theoretical model. Assume you have City A and City B that are located 10 miles apart. Each has 10,000 residents. The year is 1945 and so these cities are connected by a railroad and then a series of small, poorly-maintained "roads" (more like trails).

If you live in City A, you work in City A. In 1945, it is not likely that the frequency or the timing of the trains made commuting to City B possible. The poor condition of the trails likewise probably made trips between the two infrequent. Someone living in between these two towns -- likely a farmer, logger, hunter/trapper or a hermit -- would travel some type of slow, winding trail in order to get to town. This was also likely an infrequent trip.

This situation is pictured in my crude sketch titled "Theoretical Mobility Model: 1946".

Theoretical Mobility Model: 1946

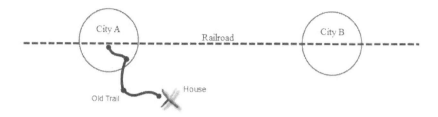

When World War II ended and we started aggressively building highways, we changed the mobility equation significantly, alla O'Toole's analysis. The railroad, with infrequent service between City A and City B, was augmented by a highway. Now, any time of day, one could take a 15 minute drive between towns. The advances in prosperity had to be immense. Business owners now had access to double the number of customers as well as twice as many employees to choose from. On the other side of the ledger, hard-working and skillful individuals had access to double the numbers of potential employers, increasing competition and wages. This is an economic advance right out of the dreams of Adam Smith and David Ricardo.

I've updated my sketch to reflect the "Theoretical Mobility Model: 1960". Note how there is no real change in the living pattern, just in the mobility options.

Theoretical Mobility Model: 1960

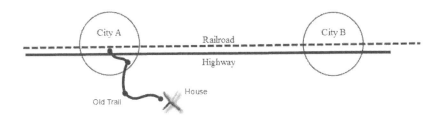

We should just pause here and note that this situation is hyper-efficient and productive. We are able to exchange goods and services back and forth and each city itself maintains a very efficient/productive pattern. This seems to be the peak of American mobility, if not in distance at least in options. Someone living in either of these cities of 10,000 can walk anywhere in their own town, can likely drive anywhere in their own town (although slowly), can visit the countryside by foot or by car and can travel between towns either by car or, less frequently, by train. For those seeking equity combined with mobility and efficiency, this theoretical model is the closest to maximizing all three.

At the risk of angering some who are turned off by such suggestions, I'll also note that this is largely the condition of European cities circa 2011. The American development pattern is uniquely American, by our choosing.

Something happens in the next incarnation that I am not going to be able to show clearly with my rudimentary sketches and that is the hollowing out of the two cities. Converting our cities from efficient and walkable to auto-centric cost untold amounts of wealth and, while it allowed (dare I say, required) us to drive more, it did little to change the prosperity/mobility equation outlined in the prior two sketches. The primary advancement was connecting the two communities. Facilitating the movement of people from a row house in town to a single-family house on the edge of town may have created short-term construction jobs and some one-time upward movement in GDP numbers, but it did not expand the market in any dramatic way. Ditto with changing the downtown restaurant to a drive through on the edge of town. These created localized, short-term construction-related spending, but did not significantly change the long-term mobility/prosperity equation.

What did change the equation was the loss of passenger rail service. I don't know exactly when this happened, but I was born in 1973 and have no recollection of rail service in my town, even though we have a huge rail yard and I have family that worked there. There are "old timers" who talk about riding the rails, but my educated guess was that this service had widely disappeared by 1980.

Again, I'll update the sketch to depict the 1980's theoretical model.

Theoretical Mobility Model: 1980

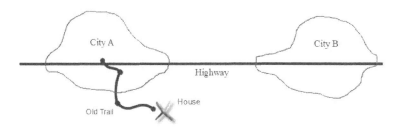

In our final "advancement", we take our lust for increasing mobility to its extreme and start connecting everything. The house in the middle of the country can now get to town taking a high-speed local street to a high-speed collector road to the highway. Because everyone drives everywhere, even for trips that used to be very local, and because we use a hierarchical road system that funnels all traffic to collector roads, the highway has to be widened.

It is easy to see how the costs of this system are so astronomically beyond our ability to pay. This is an immense amount of infrastructure to serve a population that is not proportionately greater than it was fifty years prior. Yes, we've grown as a country, but our cities have hollowed out while at the same time we've expanded into previously undeveloped areas. Were this theoretical model attached to a real city, it is more than likely that the city would have dramatically more infrastructure today (and all the costs associated with it) while actually having less population.

Now here's where I get back to the mobility question. The costs are clear to see, but where is the corresponding increment of mobility enhancement? I don't see it. Yes, by opening up land along the highway to development we've given Wal-Mart a home and produced some short-term construction jobs in the process. Sure, by putting the country home in quick commuting range of City A and City B, we've made the owner rich by allowing him to sell to a developer who will make others rich by building them a sheetrock palace that will appreciate by 15% or more each year (until the market changes and they go underwater in their mortgage), creating many construction jobs in the process. But how has this increase in mobility made us appreciably better off?

Or more precisely, what is the ultimate return on investment?

My final sketch depicts the Theoretical Mobility Model in the year 2000.

Theoretical Mobility Model: 2000

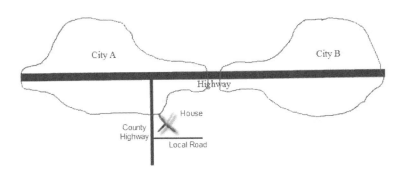

I don't quibble with O'Toole's numbers, and the arguments of mobility advocates in general, regarding the return on investment from mobility enhancements brought about by investments in the 1950' and 1960's. But since then, we have spent an untold fortune on incremental gains in the first and last mile of each trip without any obvious additional value to the macro economy. And, in the process, we've subsidized a living arrangement that has made our towns and neighborhoods financially fragile, dependent on too many variables beyond their control or even ability to influence.

If a little is good, more must be better? Not always for a Strong Town.

Mobility; We were just kidding about that.

(April 25, 2011) American transportation policy post-WW II has placed tremendous emphasis on increasing auto mobility. We have seen this in the Strong Towns examination of benefit/cost analyses, the standard approach which calculates tremendous "financial" benefits for modest savings in automobile travel time. Billions flow annually in deference to this antiquated approach. As I've also discussed, the American development pattern sacrifices a lot in the name of growth and economic development. Besides safety, ironically, one of the things most quickly sacrificed is our cherished mobility.

As a nation, have invested untold wealth in improving the first and last mile of each trip, with relatively little return. This misallocation of resources is based on a confused understanding of our experience. Essentially, we bought into the idea that, when it comes to auto mobility, "if a little is good, more must be better".

America circa 1928: A chicken in every pot and a car in every garage.

America circa 1995: A Big Mac in every hand and a paved road at the end of every driveway.

And of course, now that we've gotten used to all of this mobility, we are having a really difficult time imagining a different arrangement, even in the face of increasing fuel prices. At a recent Curbside Chat, I asked the audience how many people lived within four blocks of the place we were meeting. A few raised their hand. I asked how many of them had walked to the meeting. All hands went down.

One of my favorite examples of this myopia comes at the expense of some of my closest friends in one of my favorite small towns in Minnesota, the City of Emily. I dined often with a small group prior to planning commission meetings I used to attend there. When we are done eating and it is time to head to the meeting, everyone gets in their separate cars and drives. This is despite the fact that the restaurant is right next to the city hall where we meet - literally two hundred feet apart. In fact, it takes the others longer to drive than for me to walk. But even after I pointed out this behavioral quirk, they all still do it. It is like their DNA has been collectively reprogrammed.

Another brief digression to make the point; when I was an undergraduate, I lived fourteen blocks from the civil engineering building and walked it each day, even in the Minnesota cold. It wasn't always fun, but it was not a big deal. My first job after graduation was in my hometown. My first day of work I found out I would need steel-toed shoes and so, during lunch, I decided to walk to Mills Fleet Farm and buy some. The office building I was working in was in a suburban area, as was Mills, so when I set off walking I actually had to go along the edge of the street and then down to the end of a long block before cutting back over several hundred feet of parking lot. During the walk, no fewer than three of my new coworkers generously stopped to offer me a ride, assuming I'm sure that I was some broke college grad without a car. From then on I drove at lunch lest I appear overly needy to my colleagues.

As I indicated in the prior essay, the height of mobility in the United States really was the point in time when we connected towns with highways but had not yet turned our resources on changing that first and last mile. Our towns were now connected, but the atrophy had not begun. (Except where we had taken apart whole neighborhoods in order to build the highways themselves, although that was not atrophy but simply destruction.) At that point, the transportation network basically looked like this:

Theoretical Mobility Model: 1946

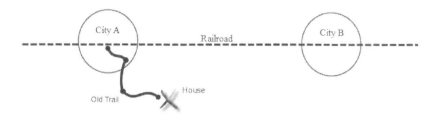

In an effort to help people clearly see the economic tradeoffs in the current development pattern, I want to demonstrate how, in pursuit of "economic development", we have actually reduced mobility.

Consider a system of three, Midwestern cities. Each is separated by six miles, the standard township grid found west of the Appalachians. When highway departments are designing, constructing and improving the highways that run between each town, they will typically set a performance benchmark for the entire corridor. In one example I recently saw, the benchmark was set at an average travel speed of 50 mph.

Theoretical Design Condition

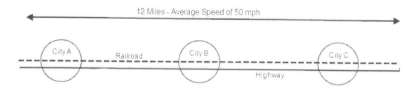

In a traditional design - one that centers on the traditional development pattern established around the railroad stop - we would have a highway that mimics the speed and efficiency of the railroad but with the added bonus of flexibility of schedule since you don't have to wait for a train. The highways would be without intersections or other speed-killing type of features and so they could be very fast and still be safe. Conversely, cities would retain their complexity and thus high-speed travel within would be dangerous. Speeds within cities would need to be very low, with a short traffic calming transition in between high and low speed zones. In our string of Midwestern towns, this is how such an arrangement would look.

City-centric Traditional Design

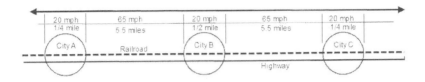

Of course, this is not how we've built anything in this country post WW II. Largely in the name of economic development, our development pattern has extended along the highways. This means a lot of intersections and complexity added to the highway system, which means that we need to lower speeds and make other improvements to handle turning traffic. Still, we tolerate a much higher accident rate than is necessary had we opted to not use our highways for economic development purposes.

When you approach the modern city, the extended development pattern means that speeds must slow even more. Ironically, states like my home state of Minnesota have mandated minimum design speeds of 30 mph and so, in the center of town, the speed is unable to be adjusted far enough downward to support the necessary complexity. This means that the complexity is removed in the name of safety, which is why highway sections don't change as they pass through town but keep their basic highway geometries. Buildings are turned to parking lots, sidewalks go unused and we basically see the atrophy take place as mentioned above.

Added together, our string of Midwestern cities evolves to look something like the following.

American Economic Development Pattern

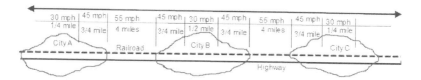

Local governments leverage the highway investment as a platform for new inducing new growth and improving economic development opportunities. I already mentioned how this adversely impacts safety -- and how we tolerate that tradeoff, despite the death toll -- but what is perhaps just as amazing is how we are also willing to accept the decrease in mobility from this arrangement. In our theoretical twelve mile stretch, the American Economic Development Pattern model takes 1 minute and 35 seconds longer to drive through than the City-centric Traditional Design.

Here are the calculations:

City-centric Traditional Design

MPH	Distance	Time (hrs)	Time (min)
20	0.25	0.01	0.75
65	5.5	0.08	5.08
20	0.5	0.03	1.50
65	5.5	0.08	5.08
20	0.25	0.01	0.75
TOTAL	**12**	**0.22**	**13.15**

American Economic Development Pattern

MPH	Distance	Time (hrs)	Time (min)
30	0.25	0.01	0.50
45	0.75	0.02	1.00
55	4	0.07	4.36
45	0.75	0.02	1.00
30	0.5	0.02	1.00
45	0.75	0.02	1.00
55	4	0.07	4.36
45	0.75	0.02	1.00
30	0.25	0.01	0.50
TOTAL	**12**	**0.25**	**14.73**

If we really wanted to improve total mobility -- even if we only measure mobility using the narrow statistic of automobile travel time -- instead of adding capacity we would spend our highway dollars closing intersections to improve speeds between towns while lowering speeds in town to restore the traditional complexity that once existed.

The fact that this approach would also saves lives while putting our country in a better financial position would simply be a bonus.

IF IT CREATES JOBS THEN IT MUST BE GOOD, RIGHT?

(January 10, 2011) At the local government level, our focus on jobs and growth obscures our understanding of the current financial turmoil as well as how we can actually create a sustained recovery. Jobs and growth are the results of a productive system, not a proxy for one. Until we reconfigure our places, sustained prosperity will remain elusive.

A large part of the Strong Towns Curbside Chat presentation is devoted to showing how our post-WW II development pattern fails to create enough revenue to financially sustain itself. We analyze real developments and compare their ongoing maintenance costs with the actual revenue they generate to show how our modern cities are financed like a classic Ponzi scheme, where revenue from an increasing number of new entrants is necessary to meet past obligations.

From the perspective of the city or town, this analysis is devastating. The whole is a sum of the parts and, when each part is running a deficit, it is easy to understand why municipal budgets are stretched beyond the breaking point. New growth may pay for itself, but only through one life cycle. After that, the costs to maintain the infrastructure dwarfs any tax revenue generated.

This analysis is also devastating to the cadre of professionals -- engineers, planners, economic developers, municipal financial advisors -- that make their living off of promulgating new growth. To them we blaspheme, challenging a belief that is nearly religious: more growth is always good. They'll respond to our analysis with something like the following:

But there is new investment, and that creates jobs and people buying stuff and all of that creates tax revenue. Your analysis is too simplistic. It is a bigger system and you don't take that into account.

To which my inner monologue responds, "How's that working out?"

I'm going to repeat a fact that makes some people quite angry, especially economic development professionals and others vested in the current system: In nearly every American city, the balance sheet does not benefit from a new job.

Local economic development officials talk endlessly about creating jobs, jobs, jobs and the need to invest in job creation. Since most American cities have no income tax, these efforts produce no tangible financial return to the city. If we spend $100,000 at the local level to create jobs, there is no basis to believe that this will ever result in $100,000 being returned to the city through new tax receipts.

But what about sales tax? Again, most cities do not rely on the sales tax for a substantial portion of their revenue. Where I live in Minnesota, cities are actually prohibited from independently enacting a local sales tax. They are only able to institute such a tax when it is approved by voters, approved by the legislature and tied for a set duration directly to a specific project. Any new jobs could generate millions and millions in sales and, except in rare instances, none of this revenue is going to be diverted to the municipal government.

Most local governments rely on property tax as their primary funding source. In a theoretical world, this should create every incentive to maximize the amount of property value while simultaneously minimizing the amount of ongoing liability -- particularly in infrastructure maintenance -- that the city assumes. In the real world, nothing like this happens. Cities fight each other -- through subsidies, waivers of regulation and other "business friendly" approaches -- for each new business, each new job, each new housing subdivision, giving little if any consideration to the long-term maintenance costs they assume.

All of this ultimately drives up local property taxes which, as any business will tell you, is not "business friendly".

Why does this happen? How can cities pursue policies that are so clearly contrary to their own long-term interests? The answer is simple: they have the incentives to do so.

The ways we have funded new growth for the last two generations cover up the true cost of our development pattern, creating the Ponzi-scheme comfort of new revenue today while postponing the day of financial reckoning, when the local government will be faced with unmanageable maintenance obligations, at least a life-cycle into the future.

In many places, we're a life cycle or more into this pattern and the growth has now stopped. Things are getting desperate, and will only get more so with each passing day. Contrary to our federal and state approach to "recovery", the answer to this problem is not more growth. The answer is a different development pattern.

Unfortunately, the entities that provide the primary incentives for the current pattern of development -- the federal and state governments -- are dealing with their own Ponzi schemes and funding shortfalls. They desperately need to lower their costs while simultaneously creating more income and sales tax revenue, local government budgets be damned. The sooner our local leaders understand that, the sooner they can stop being pawns of this system and begin to shape their own future.

There is no magical mathematical formula that will allow our cities to take on more obligations than they can support, yet remain solvent and productive places. More growth and more jobs are not the magic answers for local governments. To have a real recovery, we need a new pattern of development, one from which jobs and growth will ultimately flow. It can't be the other way around. We need to start building Strong Towns.

OUR FISCAL PROBLEMS

Lessons from a PIG

(March 23, 2011) The three most vulnerable economies in Europe belong to Portugal, Ireland and Greece, sometimes referred to as the PIG countries. You can also throw in Spain and make that a plural PIGS. These are counties where debt loads combined with slow growth and huge structural imbalances in projected budgets are causing real financial distress today.

Let's simplify this down. A country takes on debt to pay expenses. A debtor nation (like the United States along with the PIGS) will use more debt to pay the interest and then, when the principle comes due, will roll over the debt into a new loan. As with a business or a family, loans to governments are made with the assumption that the debt will ultimately be repaid. For debtor nations, there is no plan to ultimately repay the debt. Future budgets are contingent on rolling the current debt over into a future loan.

When there is no real plan to pay off the debt, lenders look even more closely at the ability of a borrower to make the payments *AND* the likelihood that they will be able to roll over the debt (that someone else will loan them the future principle and interest so they can repay the current debt). When growth is slow and when the long-term budget is hopelessly out of whack (such as when there are significant retirement commitments that have already made a claim on future principle payments), then there gets to be a concern over whether repayment is possible.

Just as with a high risk borrower on a car or with a credit card, the supply/demand of money is reflected in the interest rate. The greater the risk of default, the lower the demand for that debt and the higher the interest rate must be to attract a willing lender. For governments that have a high principle balance relative to their GDP, rising interest rates increase interest payments and further impair the ability to repay the debt. This is a downward spiral where each increase in borrowing costs compounds the problem and increases the likelihood of default.

Governments address the dual risk (missing interest payments and defaulting on the principle) by shortening the borrowing term. When you sign up for a 2 year CD at the bank, the bank will pay you a higher interest rate than if you chose the 60 day CD. The same goes for the governments. A 30-year bond will pay a higher interest rate than a 90-day Treasury bill. They have your money longer and there is more risk. So to obtain lower interest rates, debtor nations start to decrease the term over which they borrow.

You can see this play out in American debt. The following graph from Econbrowser.com[xviii] shows how the average maturity of U.S. debt has dropped from 5.8 years to 3.4 years since 1990 (the vertical axis is the average maturity in months).

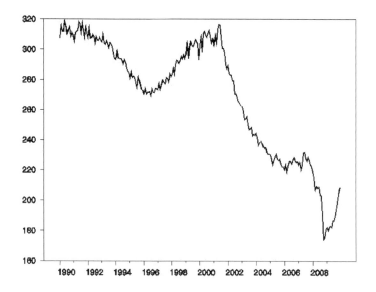

This means that we are rolling over the principle (over $14 trillion) more often. The same with the PIGS - they have to find someone to buy all of their debt each time the principle comes due, which is more and more often now that so much of it is short term. The short time frames give the debt the same feel an adjustable rate mortgage would give a homeowner.....everything is fine but we hope nothing changes before we refinance.

You can see that this is a very fragile system. There is not a lot of fallback room here.

Which is what makes the debate going on in Portugal interesting, just as the Greek and Irish debates of last year were interesting. Bond traders -- those people buying Portuguese debt -- are staying away from Portugal, which is forcing interest rates up. There is only one way for Portugal to keep rates down and that is to demonstrate that they are serious about repaying the debt. The way they do that is the new political buzzword (at least in Europe): austerity.

Austerity. Budget cuts. Tax increases. The whole living within your means thing....blah, blah, blah....

The debate going on in Portugal is over how much austerity. Right now the Prime Minister has a plan, but he is unable to get enough votes to pass it.

> *"Prime Minister Jose Socrates has said he will resign if the plan is defeated. He has said its rejection would force the debt-laden country to follow Greece and Ireland and seek an international bailout, which he opposes.*
>
> *All opposition parties have proposed resolutions calling for the rejection of the measures, which reduce pensions and state spending.*
>
> *The main opposition Social Democrats, who have previously backed austerity, have begun talking about a snap election."* [xix]

The New York Times stated the concerns of those opposing austerity, which will be familiar to any politically-aware American.

> *"But opposition parties led by the Social Democrats have said that they will not endorse further austerity measures because such measures would hurt elderly people and other vulnerable members of*

society, and could risk further delaying Portugal's return to economic growth." xx

This gets us back to our over-reliance on forecasts, especially in times of volatility. The PIGS have left themselves little room to move. If they don't adopt austerity measures and their interest rates soar, they have no cushion. They will be forced into huge, and even more painful, austerity measures or they will default (which will bring on austerity by another name). Either way, it is difficult to see how the elderly and vulnerable are spared.

The United States has an austerity measure it can take that is not available to Portugal, that being to monetize the debt. We can print money, which is something Portugal cannot do as they are part of the Euro zone and do not control the printing press. We do control ours, and so printing away our debt (such as with Quantitative Easing) is an option.

While not a tax increase or a service cut -- those would take political courage by many -- monetizing the debt can be done by unelected officials at the Federal Reserve. The result would be what is sometimes called an "inflation tax". Essentially, the debt would be repaid but your savings would be worth much less because everything would cost much more. Not very good for the elderly and vulnerable either.

So can we avoid austerity here in the U.S? Not entirely, but we have much greater flexibility than Portugal to make decisions, reach compromises, establish priorities and retool. At the local level, there is no question in my mind that we are entering a period where many of our Strong Town principles will be applied, willingly or not. It is less clear if Washington D.C. or our state capitals will be forced to do the same.

There is a sense, however, that the decisive moment is drawing near. Consider this recent quote from a Federal Reserve official as reported by CNBC:

> *"If we continue down on the path on which the fiscal authorities put us, we will become insolvent, the question is when," Dallas Federal Reserve Bank President Richard Fisher said in a question and answer session after delivering a speech at the University of Frankfurt. "The short-term negotiations are very important, I look at this as a tipping point."*

But he added he was confident in the Americans' ability to take the right decisions and said the country would avoid insolvency.

"I think we are at the beginning of the process and it's going to be very painful," he added.[xxi]

We have a lot of retooling to do, at every level of society. Do we have the courage?

Our unfaithful partner

(April 11, 2011) So many of our cities and towns rely on federal and state government spending to prop up their local finances. We inherently know and understand that these are not reliable sources of revenue, yet local leaders continue to put their communities in positions where they are dependent on that money. Local leaders today need to fully consider the implications of connecting the future of their towns and neighborhoods to such a volatile partner.

Last Friday I was doing the long ride home from Target Field, home of the Minnesota Twins, taking in the ongoing political drama on the radio. From standard talk radio to Minnesota Public Radio to one of my favorite podcasts from KCRW called *Left, Right and Center*, all the commentators were talking about was whether or not there would be a government shutdown. Likewise on Facebook when I got home. I had friends worried they would not be reporting to work on Monday and others cheering on one side or the other in this farcical game of chicken.

Now I'm sure to have offended some by calling this a "farce", but really....this latest argument was over the budget that was supposed to have been approved by October of last year. The amount of cuts finally agreed to in a budget that is estimated to be $3.8 trillion was just $38 billion. That's 1% for all you math wizards or, as they call it in Washington, a rounding error. Heck, we were off by 20 times that amount[xxii] in our projection of this year's deficit. If this is not a farce, it is unclear to me what would be.

Part of the Strong Towns Curbside Chat presentation addresses government transfer payments, the first *Mechanism of Growth* that our cities have used post-WW II[xxiii]. For two generations, our cities and towns have counted on transfers from federal and state governments to fund -- in the name of "growth" -- basic infrastructure and services like roads, streets, sewer systems, water systems, public buildings, parks, trails, sidewalks and even things like planning and engineering and, yes, even lobbying (ponder the incestuous nature of that for a while).

This is where the libertarian in me takes over because the result is so obviously destructive. We had growth, for a time, but that growth was in a pattern (suburban and auto-oriented) that was not only destructive socially and environmentally but has made literally thousands of cities across the country financially fragile, dependent on the continued flow of government money and (they hope) new growth to sustain the systems that have been created.

I can't begin to count the number of communities I have been in where the engineer prepares the report for some vital improvement and then the city mobilizes itself, not around doing the project, but around getting a grant for doing the project. And most of the time we're talking about basic maintenance.

Often the grant business itself corrupts the process. Back in my early engineering days, I had a project where it was going to cost around $300,000 to fix a leaking pipe. It needed to happen because the city's wastewater plant was about to overflow and catastrophically flood a river. Not good. But the total city budget was $150,000. That's the *annual* budget. They had absolutely no financial means to do the basic maintenance on their system[xxiv].

Unfortunately, no state or federal grant program would bother with such a small project. The answer I came up with, and was roundly applauded for, was to make the project huge. We came up with all kinds of "needed" expansions and upgrades until the total cost was $2.6 million. This was now perfect for the grant programs. The community would up taking on a $130,000 USDA loan financed over 40 years as their "fair share", politicians got some nice press releases and a grip-and-grin photo op, and the engineer (me) got a nice bonus. And the city now had all of this room for new growth. Everyone wins, right?

Working for cities and towns, I feel like they have become that caricature of the spouse that has married the philanderer, but can't bring themselves to leave. They know their spouse is lying - what they are hearing can't possibly be true - but they buy it anyway because they can't envision another possibility. They watch the games that are played and become attuned to the nuances of the errant behavior. They want to believe and make excuses when things don't go as they would in a normal relationship, but they are really in purposeful denial.

Or even worse, they aren't in denial but instead believe their spouse will change.

Here in Minnesota, Republicans have taken over the legislature for the first time in decades. Their plan to balance the budget includes cuts in local government aid. There's a catch though....the cuts are to come from cities that elect Democrats[xxv]. And the world keeps turning....

At Strong Towns we have developed ten Placemaking Principles[xxvi] - axioms to live by for those wanting to build a Strong Town. The first one is this:

> *"A Strong Town is financially stable and must not be dependent on government subsidy for the common maintenance of basic infrastructure systems."*

The current American development model is a Ponzi scheme. Without ever-increasing rates of growth -- an impossibility -- it cannot be sustained. The federal and state government is not a reliable partner, so having a plan that relies heavily on their eternal good graces is not a plan rooted in reality.

As just one more example of the unreliability of our federal partner, go back to prior essay, *Lessons from a PIG*. In that piece I wrote about how the growing federal debt is being financed more and more by short-term notes, treasuries that must be rolled over into new debt issuances every three months, as opposed to the long-term savings bonds that our grandparents used to give us for birthday presents. This short-term financing is akin to putting a large portion of our national debt on a credit card, a note increasingly payable to foreign creditors.

The current 90-day Treasury is at 0.16%, which means that a large percentage of our debt is financed at very low rates (nearly zero). Here is how that current rate compares to the rates paid over the last thirty years.

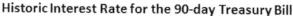

Historic Interest Rate for the 90-day Treasury Bill

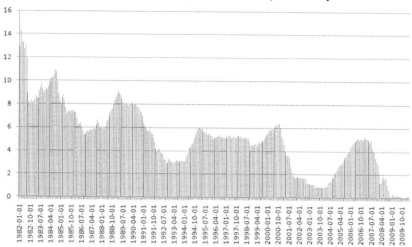

The average rate over that period of time is 5%. Okay, trusting spouse, you may want to believe that your partner is faithfully executing their duties, is faithful to your interests and generally has everything under control. So what happens when interest rates return to historical averages? What happens when we have to pay 5% on that $14 trillion? Think cutting $38 billion was hard? Try $700 billion, just in interest.

If rates follow what happened in our last big economic crisis, that of the late 1970's and early 1980's, we could be looking at 14%. That would be $2 trillion, just in interest. Good luck with that.

The finances of our towns are going to be disconnected from the finances of the federal government, at least in any positive way, whether we want them to be or not. A Strong Towns approach would be to start building local resiliency now using any federal or state assistance as money to finance the transition. The coming decades are more likely to be about contraction than growth, retrenching financially from the anomaly that was the post-WW II development pattern. That may be a tough reality to face, but face it we must.

The only thing we can really control is ourselves. Let's acknowledge the unreliable nature of our partner and turn instead to building Strong Towns.

Downgraded

(August 1, 2011) For our cities and towns, the world is changing. The stable financial system that has been the support structure of America's suburban expansion is teetering. Our places have been built and reshaped on a premise of future growth. We cling to these projections, and continue to bet our future on them, more because we can't ponder the alternative; a country without growth. Will this be the week that ratings agencies officially acknowledge what has been true for some time now?

There are two narratives the country is being given today to explain our current economic condition. Both narratives rest on the notion that what we are going through is simply one phase of an economic cycle. If you are either hyper-partisan or bristle at broad generalizations, go ahead and skip the next two paragraphs. I am neither, so I will proceed.

The first narrative rests on the idea that government is the problem. Period. Government taxes the productive parts of the economy and gives that wealth to the unproductive parts. There is excessive regulation. Government spending (except for military spending) distorts the natural order of things. We should be looking to grow our way out of the current downturn by reducing taxes, reducing government spending, cutting regulation and basically getting out of the way to let the free market work.

The second narrative rests on the idea that government is a major part of the solution. We have a lack of demand in the economy brought about by greedy Wall Street banks blowing up the housing sector. Stimulus spending saved us from going into the financial abyss. When there is a lack of demand in the economy, government needs to step in and do more. (And when times are good, government needs to step in and help those left behind). We should be growing our way out of this financial crisis by taxing those most well off and using that money to make up for the lack of demand.

Let me offer a third narrative. Ask yourself if you think this is closer to explaining reality as you experience it.

We're not in a cyclical recession or some type of downturn that will eventually fix itself. There are no set of policies that we can adopt that will put us back to "business as usual" in America. After decades of pursuing growth for the sake of growth (the common denominator of both current narratives), we've found that we've reached a point where our version of growth can no longer be sustained. Buoyed for two generations artificially by economic stimulants concocted by the left and the right, as well as a one-time fossil fuel panacea, the balloon we've floated as the "American Dream" is now coming back to earth. The only real question now is how we land.

Last week, the Department of Commerce revised downward a whole bunch of economic statistics, including GDP growth for the first quarter of this year, which is now believed to have grown at an annual rate of 0.4% instead of the less-depressing rate of 1.9%[xxvii]. Sound like a radical shift? If so, ponder this: Commerce also went all the way back to 2007 and revised that fourth quarter from -4.1% to -5.1%[xxviii]. Yes, you read that correctly. Three and a half years later and they still don't know exactly what happened.

This is the backdrop for the first of two points that need to be made about a potential downgrade of our credit rating, and it is really important to understand, especially in the context of the current debate over the debt ceiling. Regardless of whose numbers you use -- House, Senate, White House, Democrat, Republican, Tea Party, Wall Street, Commerce Department, etc... -- the projection for growth over the next ten years is an annual average of 4%. This seems reasonable when projecting from an excel spreadsheet of post WW II growth, which has been upward at more than 4% annualized, but if you don't subscribe to the two prevailing growth narratives, it seems wildly optimistic.

And if the difference between 4% and say....3% doesn't sound like much, consider this: the debt limit deal worked out yesterday after so much acrimony would cut spending by $2.2 trillion over the next ten years. The difference between a 4% and a 3% growth rate over the next ten years: $2 trillion in lost tax revenue. The difference between a 4% and a 1% growth rate is $5.6 trillion. And that is still with growth! What if Detroit, Vegas and Phoenix are not economic anomalies but canaries in the coal mine, just the weakest links in a system of growth that is inherently weak? What if we don't have growth but contraction?

The first thing to understand about this rating is that it has little to nothing to do with the debt crisis or our near-term financial position and, as such, is essentially bogus. Economists and statisticians can't accurately project the growth rate over the next three months, or even account for the growth rate from three and a half years ago, yet a difference of just one percent in our projection for the next decade will completely offset the most difficult cuts to our budget that we've made in recent times. And despite this volatility, we have a AAA rating, meaning there is the absence of all risk? Nonsense.

Put another way: there is nobody with serious money looking at the ratings agencies for advice on the credit worthiness of the United States government. The rating is an accounting check box. It does not reflect the actual riskiness of U.S. debt or our ability to repay, particularly if stressed.

That does not mean the rating doesn't matter. It matters a lot. Roughly 60% of the world's currency reserves are in U.S. dollars. Why? Because they are liquid -- there is always a market for them because the U.S. is the world's reserve currency -- and they are rated AAA, so they are accepted everywhere. For example, banks in many foreign countries are required to hold American dollars as part of their reserves. If we lose the AAA rating, these banks may have to dump their dollars and replace them with other forms of backing.

The AAA rating also creates demand for dollars from all kinds of securities and financial funds worldwide. Say you run a managed fund where the portfolio is required to maintain an average AA rating. You may have a bunch of lower-rated, riskier and higher-yielding securities, but you then blend your holdings with AAA dollar-backed debt until your total holdings average out to AA. Drop the dollar rating just a notch, and you are forced to do a massive rebalancing that will include dumping dollars into the market.

So here's the second thing to know about the credit rating: Unlike Greece, Portugal, Ireland or any other country in the world, as the United States is minting the world's reserve currency, a downgrade of our debt could be devastating. If the U.S. dollar drops and people start to unload dollars -- even slightly as part of a rebalancing -- it could have dramatic impacts just because there are so many dollars out there. When dollar-backed debt is sold into the market, there needs to be a buyer. If there are not enough buyers, only one thing can happen: interest rates will go up. That is how you get people to buy your debt; you give them a higher interest rate.

Interest rates have been at historic lows, but what if they returned to just the average rate we've experienced over the past thirty years? As I pointed out the last essay (*Our unfaithful partner*), that would add $7 trillion in interest payments over the next decade. What if the dumping of dollars brought the interest rate up over the average to the high from the past three decades? Well, then you'd be talking $20 trillion in additional interest. It makes our hard-fought cut of $2.2 trillion over the next decade look silly by comparison.

Our credit rating should have been downgraded a long time ago. When you get beyond the economist's view of debt to GDP ratio and look at the sheer volume of debt, the short-term way the debt is financed, the additional promises we have made and the obligations we have, the impossibility of growing our way out of these problems, the lack of resiliency in our economy as a whole (we import more than we manufacture in total, for example), our extreme fossil fuel dependence, and the obvious fact that we really have no plan or even a remote intention of repaying our debt but project to forever borrow more and more, how can we possibly have a AAA rating? How can we be considered "risk free"?

To me, the debt ceiling debate is silly. The constraint we have is not whether or not we are willing to borrow more money. We've put ourselves in a position where we essentially have to, as nearly every politician has said. The constraint we have is how much longer the world will be willing to lend to us. They do so now because the pass is still in the air, everyone is waiting to see where it will land and – for the moment -- there is no better place to go. But when the trickle starts -- as it could with a downgrade -- there are so many dollars out there that may come pouring back that the result is anything but predictable.

This is not the stuff of a resilient economy and not the stuff of a AAA rating. The only thing that has kept a downgrade from happening thus far is the natural human instinct to not want to be the first to shout that the emperor has no clothes.

We need to start a conversation about contraction and how to transition to a living arrangement we can actually financially sustain. It is going to look much different than the way we currently live. And, unfortunately, we should have started the transition a long time ago.

DIG BABY DIG

(October 24, 2011) Our systems for funding new infrastructure are stuck in the 1950's. Our systems for funding maintenance of existing infrastructure are not serious. Combined, these approaches create outcomes that can't be justified by a people considering themselves rational, let alone great.

Transportation for America has released a report on the state of bridges in the United States. It should be eye-opening for anyone even mildly engaged in the debate over the future of America's infrastructure. Titled "The Fix We're In For: The State of Our Bridges", the report details, in a state-by-state, county-by-county breakdown, exactly where we stand.

For example, in my home state of Minnesota, we have 1,149 bridges that have been determined to be structurally deficient, meaning they require significant maintenance, rehabilitation or replacement. According to Transportation for America, the cost to address all 1,149 bridges is $500 million. That is a sad fact by itself, but it is made ridiculous by an examination of the *Old Economy Project that Refuses to Die*, also commonly called the St. Croix Bridge.

The St. Croix Bridge is a proposed $670 million crossing of the St. Croix, a river forming the border between Minnesota and Wisconsin. The city of Stillwater has long advocated for the new bridge as a way to address their congestion problem. The current bridge, which is deficient, runs right through town while a new bridge would be on the outskirts. The nearest high-capacity bridge is eight miles away to the south.

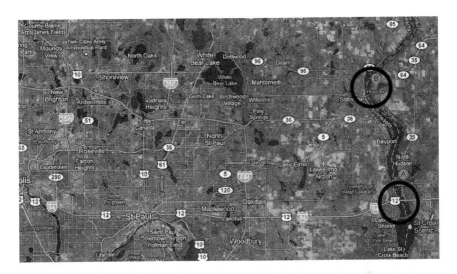

1The Stillwater Bridge (B) crosses the St. Croix river about eight miles north of the I-94 bridge near Hudson (A).

The St. Croix Bridge is a very expensive project. It is projected to cost more than the estimate for fixing **ALL** of the 1,149 structurally deficient bridges in Minnesota. The reason why this project is likely to proceed while our deficient bridges receive little funding is important to understand because it illuminates why we are in such a dire financial situation, why our infrastructure is failing and why nothing we are likely to do will make the problem better.

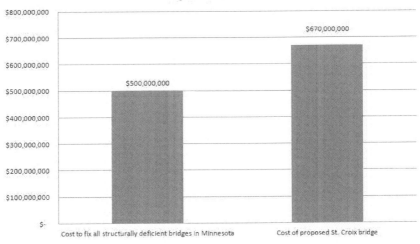

Without knowing the numbers, it would be fair to assume that the St. Croix Bridge is really critical in terms of traffic volume. Not so. The bridge is projected to carry 16,000 vehicles per day. For comparison, Minnesota's 1,149 structurally deficient bridges carry a combined 2.4 million vehicles per day.

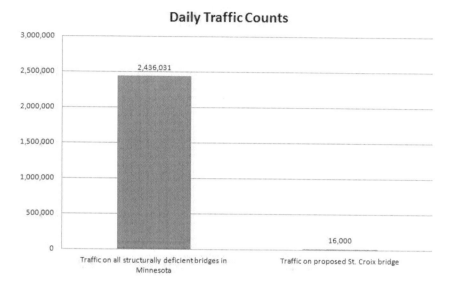

This seems insane, and it is. Why would a state full of rational people spend $670 million on one bridge to carry 16,000 cars when we already have 1,149 bridges carrying over 2.4 million cars that are in a state of critical disrepair? Why would we not spend the money first on maintaining the bridges that we have? What business do we have adding more bridges to the inventory when we do not have the resources to maintain our existing ones?

The answer is so simple and it is the key to understanding why our national infrastructure systems are in such miserable shape.

We can get money from Washington to <u>build</u> new infrastructure, but it is really difficult -- if not impossible -- to get money from Washington to <u>maintain</u> existing infrastructure.

Put simply, maintenance is a local issue. Building new -- expansion -- is something we fund out of Washington D.C. through any number of programs or appropriations. But the catch is always that the drudgery of maintenance falls lower on the government food chain. In other words, it is up to Minnesota to maintain its bridges. There is some federal money there that it can go after, but largely the existing bridges are the states' financial responsibility. The fact that there are 1,149 bridges in critical disrepair in Minnesota alone points out that this system is not working real well.

Minnesota can say no to the St. Croix bridge money, but in doing so it will not receive an equivalent amount of money that it can use to maintain its existing bridges. If Minnesota says no, the St. Croix bridge money will just go to some other state where they are willing to build something new. Neither the congestion problem in Stillwater nor the problem of the 1,149 deficient bridges will be solved. A pragmatic local politician, understanding that a new bridge solves Stillwater's problems and won't create any significant liabilities for the state for 50 years or more, makes a rational decision and supports the project. Only a handful of people reading this blog right now will be around to bear the financial burden of fixing this bridge when it someday becomes deficient.

Think that through for a second and put yourself in the place of the person fifty years from now. There will be a deficient bridge in Stillwater that will then be in need of maintenance. It will serve only a small number of cars, but the cost will be astronomical -- far more than can be afforded or that can be justified by the traffic volume. Do our grandchildren and great grandchildren put up the money to fix this bridge or do they just ignore the problem?

Well, if they follow in our footsteps, they will ignore the problem. Today we have 1,149 bridges just in Minnesota that were built generations ago that are now ours to maintain. We're not maintaining them.

And why would we? I don't ask that lightly, but simply point out that few of these bridges are high-return investments. The same thought process that is pushing the St. Croix bridge project forward was used to justify all of those other investments. We've not created any systems to ensure that these investments could be financially justified or to capture any value out of them once they were built. With the gas tax, our only incentive at the federal level is to encourage people to use more gas. Building more bridges whenever there was a congestion problem, regardless of whether or not it could be financially justified, responded to this incentive perfectly.

We're two generations into this folly. Look around and see what we've created. We have failing infrastructure everywhere. The cost to maintain it all far outstrips our ability to pay, let alone any amount we could justify spending based on the value created. We've put ourselves into enormous debt not only in government but especially at the household level just trying to keep this system going. So what do we do now?

Apparently, at least for the time being, we just keep digging the hole deeper. Dig, baby, dig.

CODING FOR PLANNER GODS

(March 2, 2011) The planning profession has a unique opportunity to examine our near-universal approach to land use regulations in the wake of a dramatic Minnesota Supreme Court decision. Unfortunately, instead of abandoning the restrictive, use-based zoning that has become ubiquitous in favor of a more permissive, form-based approach, we are going to instead codify the role of planner as local god, to the detriment of both the planning profession and the communities they serve.

When it comes to zoning, a variance (in some places called a warrant) is essentially a process whereby a waiver is granted from the code. If someone wants to build too close to the lot line than is allowed, for example, they would need to apply for and receive a variance. The ultimate decision is reserved for an appointed board or, sometimes, an elected body.

Here in Minnesota, our statutes have established a dual standard for considering variances. Inside cities, the standard is one of "undue hardship" while outside of cities it is one of "practical difficulties." For the sake of this discussion that is not a huge fact, but it is an important nuance in understanding how variances are often handled and why the Supreme Court of Minnesota has made a lot of people in the planning profession very cranky.

The "undue hardship" standard in cities requires that, for a variance to be approved, the property owner must demonstrate that the code creates a hardship that is unique to their property and that the code, as applied, would eliminate all reasonable use from their property. Taken at face value, this is an extremely high standard. An owner of a property that has been developed or used in any way for any amount of time would find it nearly impossible to argue that their prior use was not reasonable. So, in theory, few variances should be granted.

And really, there is some hard logic to that. If a 50-foot side yard setback is necessary to protect the health, safety and welfare of the community (and it must be necessary, otherwise why would it be in the code), then how can we possibly vary from that? What makes it okay to threaten the public welfare by building in that setback simply by getting a variance?

The answer, in our practical world, is that we don't treat our codes in this way. The 50-foot setback amounts to a "guideline" that, all things being equal, should be followed. If there is a good enough reason to vary from it -- for example, a property owner really wants a bigger garage -- and it doesn't offend our sensibilities (or it does offend our sensibilities but the person really, *really* wants it), then go for it. Boards of review may throw some conditions on the approval to justify their positions and force a property owner to genuflect at their power, but then it's over. Variance granted.

That is, until the Minnesota Supreme Court steps in and actually reads the law. That is what happened in Krummenacher v. City of Minnetonka, where the Minnesota Supreme Court overruled the Court of Appeals (and over 20 years of case law) by stating something that should be obvious to anyone who understands the concept of separation of powers:

> *"We [the MN Supreme Court] are unable to interpret the statutory language to mean anything other than what the text clearly says—that to obtain a municipal variance, an applicant must establish that "the property in question cannot be put to a reasonable use if used under conditions allowed by the official controls." Minn.Stat. § 462.357, subd. 6. Therefore, unless and until the legislature takes action to provide a more flexible variance standard for municipalities, we are constrained by the language of the statute to hold that a municipality does not have the authority to grant a variance unless the applicant can show that her property cannot be put to a reasonable use without the variance."*

This is a dramatic shift for Minnesota. Prior to this we had a "good guy" standard consistent with a decision titled Rowell v the City of Moorhead.

The Court of Appeals in that decision found that the words "cannot be put to a reasonable use" from the statute actually meant "if the proposed use is reasonable." And people wonder why lawyer jokes are so easy.

The fallout of the Rowell decision should have been as predictable then as the fallout from Krummenacher is today. Rowell made variances easy to get and made zoning officials very, very powerful. Essentially, the decision on what was a reasonable use became the purview of the local jurisdiction. If they found it to be reasonable, by whatever standard, it was good. For example, I personally experienced the deliberations of one zoning board that decided it was every property owner's right to have at least a three-car garage (this is Minnesota, after all), thus justifying a waiver of setback and impervious coverage limits. Zoning officials were allowed to be little Caesars, not the pizza kind but the kind that gave an arbitrary thumbs up or thumbs down to each proposal. As long as findings of fact are provided, the Rowell decision made their decision essentially unassailable.

But while Rowell made variances easy, Krummenacher goes far in the opposite direction. Here is how one planner reacted last September[xxix]:

> In the past, applicants had a good chance of getting a variance if their project was reasonable. Now, they must prove that their property would have no "reasonable use" without it -- a steep challenge.
>
> "Generally, I would have to say that [variance requests] were most always approved," said Curtis Jacobsen, director of community development for New Hope. "Applying the new standard, they would have all been denied."

Under Rowell, variances became so easy to get that the Minneapolis Star Tribune did an entire series on it last year[xxx]. Incidentally, I was interviewed for the series but took the conversation in an entirely inconvenient direction and so you will find me nowhere in the articles. My inconvenient observation: it is not the variance process but the underlying codes that are the problem.

In the Krummenacher case, the city had a 50-foot setback. The garage that was approved to be expanded was 17 feet from the property line. The important question here that nobody asks is: Why a 50-foot setback? What is the meaning of the setback? What is the purpose? Why is it 50 feet and not 25 feet? Why is it not 100 feet?

Planners reading this essay are scratching their heads. They think I've gone crazy. No, my fellow planners, it is you that have lost your bearings. We can all answer these questions together if we think about it. The answer is simple: we made it up.

There is nothing magic about 50 feet. Obviously, since the city sought fit to vary from it so the owner could put a yoga studio above their garage. There is no matter of public health or safety or welfare that demands a 50-foot setback. Chaos and anarchy will not reign if it were changed to 40 feet. Or 5 feet for that matter. So why have a 50-foot setback? Why have any setback at all?

The answer is that we have to. Our codes, which we copied from some other jurisdiction years ago, have a little box for "setback" and we have to put something there. Fifty feet sounded good for that zone. After all, those are pretty big lots. Sounds right, and we really don't get too many complaints.

The current incarnation of the planning professional, along with the myriad of codes they promote, is obsolete. We functionally have little relevance in a world where we are reduced to such foolishness as enforcing setbacks that have no discernible purpose. We discredit ourselves when we pretend they do, that somehow there is a professional skill involved in approximating acceptable distances and yields. That somehow the pattern of our places can be reduced to the functionality of a Betty Crocker cookbook, one which limits and restricts every aspect of building, unless we specifically allow it.

A cookbook in which only we are qualified to interpret. And only we, working as advisors to a group of non-professional citizens, can decide who can vary from the code, when and under what conditions.

Right now there is pending legislation sponsored by the League of Minnesota Cities, amongst others, to "fix" the statutes and provide cities a more flexible standard for variance approval. This will restore the Planner-as-God position planners all covet in their individual fiefdoms, a nearly unlimited power to decide what is right and good. This legislation will assuredly pass; it has nearly universal support, from planners and environmental advocates to builders and developers. That insight should be revealing to everyone.

To me it is tragic, however, that this moment of consequence would pass and we would not stop to consider the legacy of the standard Euclidean use-based code. We do not ponder that perhaps the statute is right - that a local code should actually regulate things of import - and that our reactionary and restrictive codes not only over-regulate, but concern themselves with all the wrong things. As planners, we've become so comfortable with a system that gives local planners and boards a tremendous amount of arbitrary and subjective power that we don't consider that maybe it should not be this way.

Maybe we should have to work harder to write quality codes instead of relying on variances to bail us out when things don't work out quite as we have planned. Maybe we need to acknowledge that we don't know so much after all, that we can't predict the future and should quit trying to do so. Maybe we should adopt a different regulatory approach, one that is market-based, permissive and based on the historic patterns that existed prior to our modern codes.

Or, we can just continue to grant variances until the budget line for "planner" is eliminated completely.

* * * * *

As a follow up note, the legislation discussed in this essay was approved unanimously by the Minnesota legislature and signed into law shortly thereafter by the governor.

DO WE REALLY CARE ABOUT CHILDREN?

(April 18, 2011) As a society, we are zealous when it comes to the safety of children. And rightfully so. Still, for some reason we find it perfectly acceptable to routinely include them in the most dangerous activity of American life: riding in a car. Even with car seats, auto accidents are the leading cause of death amongst children over two years old. It is time that child advocates start promoting mixed-use, walkable communities as an alternative to better armor and thicker padding.

I was out for a walk with my family this past weekend. My wife and I were discussing one of her friends who was expecting. This would be the second child for this friend who also has a six year old. In the conversation my wife -- who by the way I would describe as brilliant, well-informed and very frugal (I would add other adjectives, of course, but those are the ones pertinent to this essay) -- she lamented the added cost of having kids so far apart. There was a need, according to her, to essentially get all new kid "gear", from car seats to cribs.

This was puzzling to me. I'd like to think I'm a pretty modern dad, up to date on all the latest and greatest recommendations for raising happy and healthy kids, but I was not aware of a law or even a recommendation that a plastic car seat be replaced just because sixty months had elapsed since it was purchased. Looking at my six and four year old and knowing that we have not completely abandoned the idea of a third child, I started to run through the cost of outfitting an entirely new nursery. Ouch.

I'll pause here and point out that my wife is right (to which the readers say: was there any doubt?). Manufacturers of car seats are now putting expiration dates on their products - typically five to eight years - following a theory that the seat could become obsolete if a change in car design or industry norm occurred. That the practice also happens to benefit the car seat manufacturers is where I wrong-headedly took the conversation.

Actually, I went even further than that. I went all the way to the Steven Levitt and Stephen Dubner argument in SuperFreakonomics that having your kid in a car seat doesn't matter[xxxi]. Now, hold your anger at my apostasy (I heard it from my wife already) and let me explain. In the book, Levitt and Dubner statistically demonstrate that the major advancement in auto safety for non-infants was not the child seat but simply moving the kids to the back seat and putting them in a seat belt. A passenger - be they a child or an adult - is far more likely to survive a car crash if they are sitting, buckled in the back seat rather than in the front. Anyone who grew up, as I did, riding in the cab of a truck with the only restraint being the back of the driver's arm knows what I'm talking about.

This was quite the wrong argument to have with my wife, who went for the kill with this statement:

"I wouldn't compromise with our kids' safety. Would you?"

Gulp.

I wouldn't intentionally compromise on my kids' safety -- of course not -- but as I ruminated on my spousal lesson of the week it occurred to me just how often we do compromise their safety.

After perinatal conditions, which are problems that occur near or in the immediate months after childbirth, the leading cause of death amongst children ages 0 to 19 is auto accidents[xxxii]. For accidental causes of mortality, there is no close second. Even drowning, which we are militant about here in terms of baths, pools and time at the lake, is just a fraction of auto accidents. Imagine two 9/11 attacks each year that killed just kids and you still would not have the number of child fatalities America has each year from auto accidents.[xxxiii]

I take my oldest to school every day. Three days a week she is picked up, the other two she rides the bus after school. My youngest goes on many of these trips. On weekends, we drive into town for swimming lessons, grocery store runs, visits to families, trips to the park, church, movies, etc... I would estimate that my girls take between twelve and twenty trips a week. Average round trip: probably ten miles. Sure, I put my kids in car seats, make sure they are buckled according to manufacturer's specifications, drive according to posted limits, always signal my turns, etc... but what am I doing putting them in a car so often?

The answer is that I am an American and so I drive everywhere. In my town I really don't have an alternative. Even the people who live in the traditional neighborhoods have to drive out to the edge of town to get groceries.

Is this really acceptable?

If we are serious about wanting what is best for kids, shouldn't we be doing everything we can to reduce the number of auto trips people are required to take each day? And when people do take trips, shouldn't our top priority be reducing the travel speeds on local streets? Once outside of the local street network, shouldn't our top priority be the removal of the greatest source of accidents - intersections - so traffic can flow smoothly?

The best thing we can do for the safety of our children is to get them out of the car by building mixed-use, walkable neighborhoods. The safest trip is the one not taken.

So who in the child-advocacy realm is talking about this? Nobody that I can see. Safe Kids USA has all kinds of information on using your child seat, but nothing on the value of reducing trips. The National Highway Traffic Safety Administration has information on child seats, but that's it. Same with the Centers for Disease Control and Prevention and the National Transportation Safety Board.[xxxiv]

Child seats. Should they really inoculate our collective conscience?

Shortly after my oldest was born, I got in a bad accident. An oncoming car came across the lane, we glanced each other head on, I went off the road and came to a stop when Mr. Tree refused to yield. I was belted and air-bagged yet banged my head pretty hard. I could not remember my phone number, address or doctor's name and it took me a couple of months before I had my full mental cognition back. For a fast-driving, road-loving, engineer type with a new baby, this had a major impact on me.

I'm sorry if this essay has caused anyone pain. It seems we all know someone who has lost a loved one, too many of them kids, in a car accident. I don't blame any parent for doing what I do each day: buckle up the kids, give them a kiss and drive as safely as I can. Still, we need to ask ourselves, what are we really willing to risk in order to maintain the American development pattern?

Is it really worth it?

ON BEYOND INFILL

(January 17, 2011) The operating system of our development pattern - standard zoning - is not compatible with the direction that our cities need to take to remain financially viable. To rectify the massive financial imbalances suburban-style development has created for our cities, we need to make dramatically better use of the infrastructure investments we have already made. This goes far beyond the concept of infill, something standard zoning handles poorly.

Members of the planning profession that want to be considered "enlightened" by other members of the planning profession are obligated to give support to the concept of infill. Infill is the idea that we should identify gaps in the development pattern -- the places passed by -- and fully develop those prior to expanding out into undeveloped, or lightly developed, lands. To say that you support infill as a planner is to indicate that you believe these gaps should be filled first.

One reason why support for infill is a mandatory belief in the profession is because infill is thought to be the opposite of greenfield development. And greenfield development -- the expansion of the development pattern into undeveloped or lightly developed areas -- is held to be very bad. It is bad for the environment, it causes sprawl, creates auto-dependency, hurts cute little animals, yada yada yada....

The planning profession largely pays obligatory homage to the notion of infill in plans and reports, but in practice, the concept is largely discarded.

There are many reasons for this that can be summarized by the observation that infill is currently difficult to implement. There is a reason why most of those gaps in the development pattern were passed by, from difficult terrain to difficult ownership and everything in between. Greenfield development is so much easier, especially politically.

With greenfield development, typically the current owner of the site -- often a longtime resident who is simply looking to "cash out" -- lines up with the development team in a combination that is difficult for local government officials to resist. Conversely, with infill, the neighbors, who have grown accustomed to their neighborhood just the way it is, line up in logical opposition. I say "logical" because, if we're honest with ourselves, most infill projects are a variation on this obnoxious theme:

I'll suggest that there isn't anyone reading this who, if they were the occupant with a 30-year mortgage on the single-family residence pictured, would support the construction of the neighboring poverty-experiment. Infill is so logical in theory, but in practice it is anything but. That must change, and change quickly, because we need to go far beyond infill in order to make our cities financially viable.

The only analogy that comes to my mind to describe what needs to happen is theological, but since I'm writing this on Dr. Martin Luther King, Jr. day, I'll proffer it. Moses brought us the Ten Commandments, number seven of which instructs us to not commit adultery. Jesus took it further and framed this commandment for his followers, showing them how to not only read the commandment but to ingest it into their very souls, when he said in Matthew:

> You have heard that it was said, 'Do not commit adultery.' But I say to you that whoever looks at a woman to desire her has already committed adultery with her in his heart.

For a married person, committing adultery is the end of a journey that begins with having feelings for someone other than your spouse. As an instruction to his disciples, Jesus was saying that, if you want to follow the seventh commandment, don't even start on that journey. If you truly want to reach your spiritual destination, each step on your path should bring you closer to - not further from - your ideal.

When it comes to greenfield development, the planning profession lives in a world akin to Moses', where there is a commandment -- Thou shall not develop greenfields -- but an operating environment that surrounds us with every type of debauchery and enticement possible to get us to vary from this rule. Not only do we have all of the federal and state subsidies, all of the transportation spending, all of the banking, insurance, underwriting and real estate systems, and not only do we have a Ponzi-scheme, local finance system that depends on new growth, but the planning profession has one very specific tool that makes compliance with the greenfield commandment impossible.

That tool is zoning.

Our modern system of zoning, which separates everything into pods of different micro-uses and then connects each pod with a hierarchy of transportation, handles greenfield development brilliantly. That is, it is handled in a very predictable, efficient manner. On the other hand, modern zoning is brutal to infill. Small infill projects not only have to withstand neighborhood opposition, but the bureaucratic encrustation of paperwork, hearings, plan reviews and minutiae that don't scale down well, especially on sites that tend to be more challenging (the reason they are gaps in the first place).

The difficulty that standard zoning creates for infill needs to be appreciated, because infill is just the start. We need to get far beyond the concept of infill. What we need is a system of development that allows neighborhoods to establish, grow and mature over time. Single-family homes need to evolve into duplexes. Duplexes need to mature into row houses. Row houses need to grow into low rise, mixed-use flats. The operating system of our cities needs to allow places to mature in this way. It needs to be easy, intuitive and - most of all - desired by everyone involved.

In other words, it is not enough to simply say, "Thou shall not develop greenfields," but then continue to operate in a system where greenfield development is the natural conclusion of nearly every journey. If we agree that greenfield development is bad, then we need a radically different mode of operation. We need a new operating system, and that begins with a national book burning to rid ourselves of our destructive zoning codes. (Politically speaking, I strongly suspect that such an event would be a bi-partisan affair.)

Now, do we at Strong Towns suggest there should be neighborhood anarchy? Of course not. We need an operating system for the future of our neighborhoods. The best place to start would be the SmartCode or similar form-based alternative. In a form-based code, we see regulations that are permissive (state what they want) and not restrictive (state what they oppose), address primarily the form the property takes and not the use, create a predictable development pattern that is compatible with existing neighborhoods and streamline the bureaucracy to make approvals quick and easy.

The key insight about form-based codes, however, is how they create a pattern of development where neighborhood growth is positive for the people already living there. Since all form-based growth builds on the existing pattern of the neighborhood, new development is not a threat to the current order but instead, by definition, enhances it. As our neighborhoods mature in a form-based operating system, gaps are filled in, then places are connected, then destinations are naturally created and, over time, expanded and enhanced. There is no step backwards in a form-based system, just forward.

If we don't want greenfield development -- and at Strong Towns we agree that it has little redeeming value, especially as society is starting to comprehend the financial impact of two generations of horizontal growth -- we need something more than a commandment that few follow. We actually need a different path to follow, an entirely different operating system that will continuously make our cities stronger. That is what it means to build Strong Towns.

WHEN MONEY DIES

(July 18, 2011) As a country, we are desperate to prop up the American suburban experiment, to "get America working again". The non-negotiable American way of life, the standard of living most of us have and even feel entitled to, has been revealed to be more fragile than we would ever have imagined. How far will we go to sustain the unsustainable?

I spent last week on vacation and, as with any good vacation, got a chance to catch up on some reading. Amongst some lighter reading, I finished off Adam Fergusson's *When Money Dies: The nightmare of deficit spending, devaluation, and hyperinflation in Weimar Germany*. Now before I get anywhere near apocalyptic-sounding, I want to make clear that I do not consider USA circa 2011 to be equivalent to Germany circa 1923. While the threat of hyperinflation is here, it remains but a remote possibility. I do not predict the chaos and calamity of post-WW I Germany for us. That being the case, the book was chilling and gave me a lot to think about.

Coming off of World War I, Germany was forced to sign a treaty that, amongst other things, required it to make large reparation payments to the Allied forces. It is a misconception that it was these payments alone that caused the inflation -- that Germany simply printed money to pay their debt. The payments to the Allies were to be made in gold. Despite the remarks of our Federal Reserve chairman last week that holding gold is simply "tradition" and that gold is not currency[xxxv], the metal has value across societies and, as we will see in a minute, is what ultimately provided Germany with a backstop for a stable currency.

While the reparations were a tremendous burden, the inducement for inflation was domestic. Having spent and borrowed heavily to finance the war, Germany, as the loser, had no spoils (neither did France or England, in this case, since victory was an armistice and not a plunder). The German government owed their own population tremendous amount of money since it was their own citizens buying government bonds that was largely used to finance the war. To pay this back, they literally just printed money. They started up the printing press and they printed, and printed, and printed money until everyone was paid back.

Of course, this is not a far cry from where we are today. We've financed multiple wars (engagements, presidential actions, etc....) while bailing out banks and insurance companies, doing record stimulus spending, creating a new trillion dollar entitlement, paying out record unemployment and other household assistance and preparing for the pending retirement of America's largest generation. Since 2008, the Federal Reserve has created and injected $5.3 trillion into the economy, much of this given to the U.S. Treasury to finance the national debt. The exact mechanism is that the Fed buys treasury bonds so, in theory, they will get that money back in the future.

Of course, getting that money back will happen when the time is right, when the economy is back booming again. We all remember (not) how, during the dot.com boom or the housing boom, our treasury was so flush and our population so fat and happy that we were willing to tax ourselves more and cut back on our spending to pay off our debt. This is the situation Germany found itself in as well, only they were actually not fat and happy. They were desperate. And so they printed more money. Lots more.

I don't remember the entire Weimar Republic hyperinflation episode as more than one or two lines in my history book, crammed in between the two great wars, but the fascinating thing about this book was how long it took to happen and what the transition was like. At first, the inflation solved a lot of problems. Yes, prices went up, but relatively speaking debt -- the bigger burden at the time -- went down. To quote the book:

> *"With inflation alone....can a government extinguish debt without repayment, or wage war and engage in other non-productive activities on a large scale: it is still not recognized as a tax by the tax-payer."*

The reason for this is that the majority of people did not feel poorer. Rising prices were a burden, but wages were rising too. Imagine you make $50,000 this year but next year you get a raise and make $75,000. Even if gas and food prices double, you're going to feel a little better off.

As things went on, the dog kept chasing its tail, and the Reichsbank kept printing money. The government, unable to balance its budget, and unable/unwilling to really tax its people, simply printed its way to solvency. They paid wages and benefits to people largely with printed money. They spent money on programs and infrastructure via the printing press. The objective of the government at the time was full employment, and stimulating the economy through government spending of printed marks was how they accomplished it. Of course, if it were only that easy. From the book:

> *"In the inflationary period new factories were built, old establishments reorganized and extended, new plant laid down, participations in all fields of industrial activity bought up, and the great amorphous concerns founded. Too late, it was found that this process had undermined the capital structure of the country: capital was frozen in factories for which, because of the extermination of the rentier and the reduction of the real wages of so many of the great consumer classes, there was no economic demand. Once the demand for goods was shut off and the flow of cash dammed, the fate of productive apparatus was sealed."*

This eerily sounds like America today where, instead of industry, our inflated capital was pumped into the suburban experiment. There it sits frozen, that is, only where it has yet to vanish altogether, for there are few buyers and many sellers now. We're trying to prop it all up -- we've yet to hit the bottom -- but it is getting harder and harder to do.

This is because, as with Weimar Germany, more and more people are being caught on the wrong side of the inflation game. You've had your wages increase from $50,000 to $75,000 (a 50% increase), but your cost of essential items like energy and food doubled (a 100% increase). That may work for a year if you make $50,000 to start, but not if you make $20,000. That lower wage earner soon finds their wages not keeping up with just the essentials of life. As time goes on and inflation continues, progressively higher and higher wage earners are put in the same situation.

In the U.S., wages have been stagnant for a decade. The stagnation was offset by rising housing prices and the get-rich-quick action in the suburbs. And, of course, the most leveraged and least resilient amongst us are the first to feel the effects.

Over time, as prices kept rising faster than wages, some crazy things happened. Workers started to demand to be paid at the end of each day. There were stories of people ordering dinner at one price and then, because of the rapid inflation, having to pay a different price when dinner was over. Large purchases like new cars became impossible as a 20% down payment would be near worthless two months later when the purchaser was to take possession.

People were desperate to tread water, to simply hold onto what they had. They would leave work after getting their wages and go out and buy anything they could find, knowing that whatever tangible item they could purchase could later be sold or traded for a higher value. "Growth" was created because people invested their wealth wherever they could, lest they hold onto their money and watch its value disappear. From the book:

> *"As the old virtues of thrift, honesty and hard work lost their appeal, everybody was out to get rich quickly, especially as speculation in currency or shares could palpably yield far greater rewards than labour. While the anonymous, mindless Republic in the shape of the Reichsbank was prepared to be the dupe of borrowers, no industrialist, businessman or merchant would have wished to let the opportunities for enrichment slip by while others were making hay. For the less astute, it was incentive enough, and arguably morally defensible, to play the markets and take every advantage of the unworkable fiscal system merely to maintain one's financial and social position.*
>
> *As that position slid away, patriotism, social obligations and morals slid away with it. The ethic cracked. Willingness to break the rules reflected the common attitude. Not to be able to hold on to what one had, or what one had saved, little as it worried those who had nothing, was a very real basis of the human despair from which jealousy, fear and outrage were not far removed."*

While early on the dollar would trade for 5 marks, by the end it fell to one dollar for 4,200,000,000,000 marks, the entire economy reduced to barter and foreign currency. Unemployment spiked as the inflation-driven investments were revealed for what they were: worthless.

As I said earlier, while the pace picked up at the end, this decline all happened over many years. There were a number of opportunities that politicians and others had to put the brakes to this disaster. Nobody could. This also eerily has a tinge of our current political situation. From the book:

> *"Much as it may have been recognized that stability would have to be arranged some day, and that the greater the delay the harder it would be, there never seemed to be a good time to invite trouble of that order. Day by day....the reckoning was postponed, the more (not the less) readily as the prospective consequences of inflation became more frightening. The conflicting objectives of avoiding unemployment and avoiding insolvency ceased at last to conflict when Germany had both."*

We can see ourselves in many ways in that fear of the tough reckoning. While many politicians talk tough, they reflect our unease. Are we really prepared to deal with the suburban malinvestment of the past two generations? Are we prepared to undergo the difficult transformation in our living arrangement and the massive decline in our standard of living required to face up to our core insolvency and lack of productivity? Knowing that we aren't helps us see that the German policy of inflation -- kicking the can down the road -- was not so crazy at the time.

Even so, the result is no less predictable. From the book:

> *"What really broke Germany was the constant taking of the soft political option in respect of money. The take-off point therefore was not a financial but a moral one; and the political excuse was despicable, for no imaginable political circumstances could have been more unsuited to the imposition of a new financial order than those pertaining in November 1923, when inflation was no longer an option....Stability only came when the abyss had been plumbed, when the credible mark could fall no more, when everything that four years of financial cowardice, wrong-headedness and mismanagement had been fashioned to avoid had in fact taken place, when the inconceivable had ineluctably arrived."*

As a final thought here, it was also important to note in this book that, as the tough decisions got put off further and further, the solutions obviously became more difficult. As the needed medicine became more distasteful, the politics of the day became more extreme. In Germany of 1923, you had the communists on one side and the national socialists on the other. Their numbers grew as the situation became more desperate, as the pragmatic kick-the-can strategies simply put off and compounded the inevitable reckoning. The communists were for the worker, the Nazis for the industrialists. In the end, the workers lost their jobs and the industries all went bankrupt.

> *"Inflation is the ally of political extremism, the antithesis of order. At other times - in post-revolutionary Russia, in Kadar's Hungary - it may have been deliberately engendered in order to destroy the social order, for chaos is the stuff of revolution. In Germany at this time, however, the inflationary policy was the consequence of financial ignorance, of industrial greed and, to some extent, of political cowardice. It therefore produced hothouse conditions for the greater and faster growth of reactionary or revolutionary crusades."*

Of course, we know how that all tragically ended in Germany.

We have a lot to ponder in this country. A lot to discuss. And we have a lot of really difficult decisions to make. It will be politically easier in the near-term to continue to debase the currency, to pretend that we are making good on all of our obligations while continuing to expand our empire, with inflation providing the illusion of prosperity. It will be very tempting to restart the suburban experiment by resetting our private debt levels through inflation. Is this just postponing the inevitable?

Incidentally, after Germany had *"plumbed the abyss"* they restored their currency by a) stopping the printing press, and b) issuing new currency that was fully backed by and exchangeable for gold. For the United States, the fragility of our suburban experiment is compounded by our experiment with fiat currency (we went off the gold standard in 1971). Never has the world held one reserve currency that was not backed by anything but "good faith and credit."

We may need more of both soon enough.

* * * * *

A further note: After I originally published this essay I was hit with a backlash from a few individuals who claimed that Adam Fergusson was a right wing radical and that the book I referenced was a right wing cult classic. Whatever.

I had independently searched for a book on the hyperinflation of the Weimar Republic because I had heard so many people refer to it and, quite frankly, I didn't think these talking heads fully understood the history. I simply wanted to know more. This book was excellent, was a factual history free of propaganda or any references to the present and I highly recommend it for anyone who has research desires similar to mine.

What was most haunting and provided me the most instructive insight was the realization that inflation is a tool of the elite and that it's most savage impact is on the poor. That came through clearly throughout the text.

It should also be stated that the only place in America I hear calls for additional quantitative easing – the modern version of money printing -- is in the CNBC/Wall Street echo chamber.

COMPLETE STREETS

Co-opting Complete Streets

(May 16, 2011) The idea of a Complete Street is compelling in almost every way, but when the engineering profession begins to adopt it wholesale, we need to pause and look at the outcomes. Are we getting Complete <u>Streets</u> or are we getting Complete <u>Roads</u>? The difference is tremendous and will impact the financial viability of an approach to building places that is long overdue.

The Complete Streets concept is one that is long overdue. We've spent two generations transforming a public realm once comprised of walkable, mixed-use neighborhoods into auto-only zones. These are places where the kids used to play ball in the street. Today a kid can't even play safely in their own front yard.

At Strong Towns, we've worked to illuminate the fact that this transformation has been done at tremendous financial cost. This is not only because the construction of wider, flatter and straighter streets has been expensive, but because the auto-centric nature of the transformed public realm drives private-sector investment out of traditional neighborhoods, dislocating it to places that provide more buffering to the car.

Not only that, but the redevelopment that has happened in these traditional neighborhoods has largely been on a suburban framework, using the parking ratios, setbacks and coverage restrictions of modern zoning to reduce density (and the rate of return). Financially, these traditional neighborhoods are largely insolvent, lacking the tax base to support the maintenance of their basic infrastructure.

Enter the concept of a Complete Street. To me, the fundamental contribution of Complete Streets to the discourse surrounding the future of our towns and neighborhoods is the recognition that our streets must serve more than just cars and that the public realm can no longer be an auto-only zone. The fact that the Complete Streets model has broken the stranglehold that the auto-only design mentality has had on our streets should be the cause of unending rejoice.

In March I was able to have dinner with Kaid Benfield. During the course of our conversation, he enlightened me on how the Leadership in Energy and Environmental Design (LEED) standards were tweaked with Neighborhood Design principles. The result, LEED-ND, takes a great concept -- buildings that are energy efficient and environmentally friendly -- and overlays it on a development framework that reinforces these principles. In other words, no more "green" buildings in the middle of a greenfield, with 30 mile commutes each way.

In a similar vein, I'm going to now, humbly, suggest a way in which the Complete Streets concept can evolve to achieve what I believe is its principle intent, that being Complete Neighborhoods.

I've now seen two projects where engineers promoted the use of "complete streets". In each I see the engineering profession co-opting the Complete Streets moniker without any thought to a Complete Neighborhood. For the engineers on these projects, the approach remains the same. I'll quote from my 2010 essay, Confessions of a Recovering Engineer:

"An engineer designing a street or road prioritizes the world in this way, no matter how they are instructed: Traffic speed, Traffic volume, Safety, Cost

The rest of the world generally would prioritize things differently, as follows: Safety, Cost, Traffic volume, Traffic speed

In other words, the engineer first assumes that all traffic must travel at speed. Given that speed, all roads and streets are then designed to handle a projected volume. Once those parameters are set, only then does an engineer look at mitigating for safety and, finally, how to reduce the overall cost (which at that point is nearly always ridiculously expensive)."

One of the places I've seen Complete Streets applied is *My Hometown's Last Great Old Economy Project* (also known as College Drive). In this instance, the design starts with a minimum design speed and a projected traffic volume, the latter being the stated impetus for the project. In the current design framework, this analysis mandates four lanes of fast-moving traffic. The engineers then move on to the "safety" criteria and then -- if we can afford it -- we accommodate bikes and pedestrians. This is done, of course, at tremendous cost - estimated at over $7 million for a mile of road.

Now notice that I called this route a "road" and not a "street". Understanding the difference between a <u>road</u> and a <u>street</u> is critical to understanding the problem we have with engineers misusing the Complete Streets approach. From the Placemaking Principles for a Strong Town:

> *"To build an affordable transportation system, a Strong Town utilizes roads to move traffic safely at high speeds outside of neighborhoods and urban areas. Within neighborhoods and urban areas, a Strong Town uses complex streets to equally accommodate the full range of transportation options available to residents."*

Roads move cars at high speeds. Streets move cars at very slow speeds. We should build roads outside of neighborhoods, connecting communities across distances. We should build streets within neighborhoods where there are homes, businesses and other destinations. The auto-road is a post-WW II replacement of the rail-road. The street should be what it has always been; the street.

The fundamental design flaw of the post WW II development pattern -- the false premise upon which every other design tragedy has been committed -- is the transformation of our streets into roads.

High speed auto travel has no place in urban areas where the cost of development demands a complex neighborhood pattern with a mixing of uses, multiple modes of travel and a public realm that enhances the value of the adjacent properties. High speed traffic destroys value within our neighborhoods. It drives out investment. There is no amount of pedestrian enhancement that we can build to offset the negative response people have to being in the close proximity of speeding traffic.

Without aggressive traffic calming -- which is part of the Complete Streets playbook -- we will simply be building Complete Roads. A Complete Road will not transform the public realm, no matter how much money we put into *accommodating* pedestrians and bikers with bridges and tunnels. A Complete Road will not attract significant private-sector investment in the key neighborhoods where we have so much existing infrastructure liability. And a Complete Road will cost a fortune, without changing the insolvency problem facing our cities.

If there is one thing our current financial situation should teach us about the engineering profession it is this: engineers will bankrupt us if given the chance to build our cities and towns the way they envision them. It is predictable that the engineering profession will embrace the concept of a Complete Road -- which is nothing more than a bad design made politically correct by throwing an expensive bone to bikers and pedestrians -- because it fits with their hierarchy of values (speed, volume, safety and then cost). Insidiously, promoting Complete Roads will ensure them more funding than they would otherwise receive. You can call them "streets" all you want - unchecked, they are going to build "roads".

I love Complete Streets. They are essential to a Strong Town. Let's get out there and build them, but make sure the engineers don't con you into a Complete Road. Demand slow cars and a Complete Neighborhood to go along with your Complete Street.

A complete road

(May 17, 2011) Yesterday's essay about the difference between a Complete Street and a Complete Road was screaming for an example. Here is the Complete Road section being used by my hometown of Brainerd, MN, for *My Hometown's Last Great Ola Economy Project.*

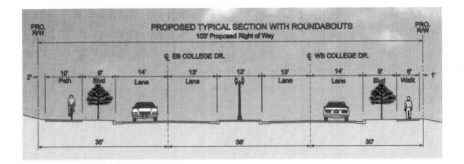

Yes, this section has a dedicated bike path. And yes, this section also has a dedicated walking path. Throw in some decorative lighting and trees and you have yourself a Complete Street. Right?

Not really. Take a look at those driving lanes. There are two lanes in each direction, one that is 14 feet wide and the other at 13 feet. Those are highway dimensions used for high speed travel. Thus you have a Complete Road, the dream of every engineering contract.

Right now, students that live on one side of this road routinely get in their cars and drive to the college on the other side of the road. I know - I went there for a spell. That and they don't even bother to shovel the walks when it snows because nobody uses them. And that is with the current road, which is *narrower* than the new proposal. I don't care if they do build a pedestrian bridge or a tunnel, nobody is going to cross this street using anything but a car.

And because of that, there will be no intensification of the development around this corridor. No private-sector investment. No urbanism. This is simply a monster dump of money for one purpose: to move more cars, more quickly. The bike path and walking path, in this application, are just expensive ornamentation that will be little used. People -- and money -- will generally flee from this auto-centric corridor.

So how do we make it better? How do we make this Complete Road into a real Complete Street with a corresponding Complete Neighborhood?

My recommendation to the city was that they make this a two-lane street. With roundabouts at the key college entrances, traffic would flow just fine, albeit much slower than it does today. Such a design, with 10-foot lanes, would be easy for pedestrians to cross, especially with a nice, wide median and periodic jut-outs of the median and walk to shorten the distance people have to cross. You could put large walks along both sides and they would actually be used as the slow-moving cars would not threaten pedestrians. You could also skip the bike lanes as the bikes could actually ride right in the traffic stream. Imagine that!

And not only would my alternative cost millions less, but it would provide a platform that would connect the tremendous housing demand from students and professors with the underdeveloped and declining neighborhood on the opposite side of the street. In other words, there would be a reason to invest there because there would be a reason to live there.

But even if engineers insisted on a four-lane design, 10-foot lanes are more than adequate for the speeds you are going to want through this section. Going to 10-foot lanes would save a full 14 feet of bituminous width, the cost of cutting one entire lane, not to mention all the money the city had to spend acquiring land and easements to accommodate such a wide section.

Ah, but what about the cars? They'll be so unsatisfied if it takes them an extra 37 seconds to travel this stretch of road. A pity, indeed.

Spend less money. Get more return. That is the essence of a Strong Towns approach. I'm just grateful that this will be the last of these mega-projects my hometown will be able to afford. I only wish we were using our final hoorah on something more productive and beneficial to the community.

CONSOLIDATION

Consolidation is the wrong response

(May 2, 2011) Consolidation is the current least-painful way to avoid dealing with the underlying financial problems of our cities and towns. But like consolidation in the banking sector, municipal consolidation will only amplify the underlying fragilities in our development pattern. A better solution would be to embrace the innovations — and failures — that would come from thousands of local experiments in adapting to our current financial situation.

Our state and local governments are in a pickle. The gravy train from Washington — which was not all that great, really — has stopped running. The good old days — which were not all that good, really — are long gone. "Recovery" seems a distant dream. And on top of it all, the electorate seems mad as hell and unwilling to wait for any type of long-term "transformation" to take place. What's a decent local politician to do?

The first thing to try is to borrow money, spend the rainy day fund and cook the books a little, hoping this whole thing will blow over soon. Been there and done that.

The next thing is to borrow seriously more money, try some "stimulus" in the form of more spending and/or less taxes, and basically inject some adrenaline into the heart of the economy to try and bring it back to life.

Now we are at the point where we start to talk about changing the way we do things. In other words, we've come kicking and screaming into the "transformation" phase. But this is the early transformation phase, that part of the cycle of decline where we try and change without really having to actually change. And what better way to make non-substantive change than consolidation?

Consolidation is a response to the notion that our problem is essentially one of efficiency. The idea is that local governments are not efficient enough; therefore, we can increase efficiency by combining them into fewer governments. Like the banking sector, having fewer players creates more efficiency.

And like banks, fewer players will amplify fragility.

Take school consolidation as an example. Consolidating schools is something that has been going on since the early 1900s, but it became one of the "solutions" to the budget problems of the late 1970s and early 1980s. And while there is little argument that consolidation of schools allows for greater efficiency, it comes at a cost.

Many of today's school districts are geographically huge, especially in rural areas. Increased size means more bureaucracy and more red tape, increasing the distance between teacher and administrator, between classroom and parent. Multi-million-dollar bonds to construct large, centralized facilities made more sense before $4 gas. The reality today is that, no matter how high fuel costs go, we'll be busing kids for miles each way, unable to walk away (no pun intended) from these massive investments we've made. We have exploding childhood obesity and, again, no way to avoid forcing our children into hours of sedentary bus riding each day.

Most important, by consolidating schools we traded innovation for efficiency. In a day when we desperately need innovation in how we educate our kids, our school systems seem calcified, unable to change course in any substantive way, even as we fall behind in many key areas.

The need for innovation is the key reason we should not be seeking the consolidation of local governments.

Lack of efficiency is not our problem. Lack of innovation is. And not the type of innovation that saves a few dollars buying paper clips in bulk. What we need is the type of innovation that provides different responses to the same stresses.

Our biggest problem as a nation right now is that our places are generally all vulnerable to the same things. That is because we have all used the same cookbook and the same mechanisms of growth (government transfers, transportation spending and debt) to get here. Fundamentally, our cities are all pretty much the same. When gas prices rise, our cities struggle. When growth slows or stalls, our cities go into decline. When government aid goes away, our places start to implode. Consolidation will only cover up this lack of resilience, and the day of reckoning will be pushed off and made more difficult as a result.

Instead of consolidation, we should embrace the core strength of America: an ability to innovate. This means loosening the controls we have placed on our cities and towns, thus allowing local officials to try different solutions to the problems they face. The correct response is not to become more parochial, it is to become less.

So why can't we do this? The reason is clear: We can't deal with failure. We hear the report about the one city that does something really stupid and we rush to pass legislation to ensure it never happens anywhere again. We see a senseless policy outcome and we create all kinds of rules to deal with it. We see a city near failure and we feel obligated to bail it out. We have no mechanism to wring success out of failure.

But clearly, if we want innovation, we have to embrace failure. After all, what percentage of businesses fail? What percentage of species fail? Natural systems, like economic systems, evolve, adapt and create only in an environment where failure is allowed. If we want innovation, we have to allow failure.

Does this mean we have to let some cities fail? Yes, but that need not condemn a percentage of our people to live in ruin. What if we took failing cities and put them in a sort of receivership? What if we gave a bonus to the communities that were most successful if they agreed to "adopt" one of the failing communities and walk it through a restructuring? This is just one idea. There are more.

Consolidation will not get at the core problems our cities face. If we want to build resilience and find solutions to our problems, we need to embrace the chaos — the innovation along with the failure — of natural systems, and create a framework where local governments can experiment with different responses to the current crisis.

Little Bets

(September 5, 2011) Is the challenge facing our local governments one of efficiency -- do they lack the systems to make good use of resources -- or is it one of innovation? If it is efficiency, then consolidation can address those problems. But if what we need is more innovation, we have to find a way to unleash local governments to make little bets - low risk experiments in solving problems.

We are comfortable with the notion of consolidation here in the United States, especially in times of financial difficulty. When big airlines get in trouble, two of them will merge together with talk of efficiency and elimination of duplicating services. When the big banks got in trouble in 2008, the Federal Reserve and U.S. Treasury encouraged J.P Morgan to buy Bear Stearns and Bank of America to acquire Merrill Lynch. Again, the talk was all about how the new, larger entity could leverage resources for efficiency gains. We see this repeated in auto companies, telecommunications and media conglomerates as well. Bigger is better.

Or is it? If there is one thing that airlines, auto companies and telecommunication companies seem to have in common here in the United States it is a lack of innovation. For the latter, anyone who has been outside of the country and marveled at the ubiquitous cellular service can attest that we have terrible coverage here in the United States. When General Motors failed it was widely acknowledged that they were building an inferior product. And while we may get innovation in the too-big-to-fail banks, it is typically of the swindling variety.

If consolidation creates efficiencies, the tradeoff is that the bureaucracies become bigger, more entrenched and less likely to be naturally innovative. Where companies have overcome this -- for example, a company like Google or a Minnesota example like 3M -- they have typically walled off departments into a company within a company or placed a very high value on individual experimentation. Google, for example, asks their engineers to devote 20% of their time to their own projects. But most companies are not Google. Or even 3M.

The fact that no local government runs like a company has not kept politicians from talking about consolidation as a big part of the answer for tight budgets and failing towns. While I'm aware of the rumblings here in Minnesota, where the state proscribes the taxing policy and spending approach for all cities, a quick search revealed many places where consolidation is being discussed.

In Rhode Island, the state has set caps for local government spending increases while at the same time increasing mandates and cutting aid (a sadly familiar story). When too many cities requested waivers of the cap, people like Dr. Edward Mazze, a professor from the University of Rhode Island, suggest consolidation as the answer.[xxxvi]

> *Mazze said the state should go back to the drawing board, arguing that it might be time to once again consider some form of consolidation.*
>
> *"The cap made sense in good times but in today's economy, the cities/towns need to fend for themselves," he said. "It is time to do away with the caps and allow voters on a local level to determine more taxes or less services. The solution to this problem is to rethink the type of government structure and services that Rhode Islanders want and can afford."*
>
> *Mazze said a five county government could save millions of dollars for taxpayers.*
>
> *"Can a state with one million people afford 39 cities and towns? This is the time to look at a five county government with one school superintendent, one police chief, one fire chief, one maintenance department per county," Mazze said. "We would be able to save dollars, have a more efficient system of governing, retain and attract more businesses and have lower property taxes."*

Anyone ever run into an incompetent superintendent? How about an ineffective police chief? Ever heard of a corrupt public official? I digress....

In New Jersey there is a 501(c)3 organization that has been established to advocate for consolidation. They recently issued a guide for cities looking to go through the consolidation process called Courage to Connect.[xxxvii] Governor Chris Christie has signed legislation making it easier for towns to consolidate.

> *"It's absolutely ridiculous that New Jersey has 566 redundant municipalities,"* said Gina Genovese, the executive director of Courage to Connect New Jersey and one of the book's three authors. *"We all have to work together, we have to make a sustainable structure."*

A book from Peter Sims called *Little Bets: How Breakthrough Ideas Emerge from Small Discoveries* reveals an alternative to consolidation. While the book never even mentions government, the concepts are powerful and would transfer well, especially at a time when reform and innovation is so badly needed. The notion of placing "little bets" -- tiny experiments in innovative approaches, many that will fail but some that will pay off -- is something consistent with American culture. From a review of the book[xxxviii] :

> *The word "innovation" seems perilously overworked these days, invoked by corporate leaders and earnest politicians eager to signal progress and express faith in our ability to solve problems and improve the world. We're always ready to endorse the concept, though applying it may be another story. "I'll be happy to give you innovative thinking," a bedraggled employee tells his boss in a classic Leo Cullum cartoon. "What are the guidelines?"*
>
> *Guidelines are what Peter Sims seeks to provide in "Little Bets," an enthusiastic, example-rich argument for innovating in a particular way—by deliberately experimenting and taking small exploratory steps in novel directions. Some little bets will not pay off, of course, in which case little is lost; but others may pay off in big ways.*

At the local government level, we don't have a lot of innovation going on. We have competent and less-than-competent management, but we don't have innovation. That is not because our people are not innovators. It is because states typically mandate, regulate and manage affairs at the local level to the point where only a narrow band for innovation typically remains.

Consolidation is a response to inefficiency. At the local level, inefficiency is not our problem. Lack of innovation is. We have the same template of codes, regulations, budget approaches, software, staffing, street standards, policies, etc... in nearly every city in the country. Who is truly innovating out there?

As we go through this great transition, as a society we really need to clarify what we expect from local governments. Do we expect them to operate as utilities, essentially do a few, simple things well and leave it at that? Or do we expect them to take on more. Do we expect them to be the front line for developing new solutions to the problems we face?

If we want the utility approach -- efficient but dumb -- then we need to strip away much of the responsibility we have given local governments and simplify their responsibilities down to just a few. Let them plow streets, mow grass, run park programs, collect water bills and run elections. Leave all the planning, zoning regulations, infrastructure investments, economic development and tax matters to someone else.

But if we are going to demand more from cities, then we need to get out of the way and let them become platforms for innovation. We need to remove the mandates (go ahead and replace them with measurable outcomes). We need to get rid of the parochial regulations. We need to allow local governments to experiment with different approaches knowing that many of them will not turn out well but that some of them will. Those that do will create the innovations for everyone else to adopt, customize and improve upon.

That is how little bets can create big change.

SUBURBAN SALVAGE

(October 10, 2011) What is the future of the structures built during the Suburban Experiment? While it is unsettling for many to even consider, it is likely that a high percentage will be used for salvage material. Acknowledgement of this by Americans is not a sign of failure but an indication that we can be a thoughtful and resourceful people. Present times call for nothing less.

Last week I was interviewed by a number of reporters about the conclusions and recommendations contained in the *Curbside Chat Companion Booklet*. There was one question that kept coming up that I was not really prepared for: *What is going to happen to all of the stuff we've already built?* It's not like I haven't thought a lot about it -- I certainly have -- but more that the way things came out of my mouth in answering it were not coherent enough.

Or perhaps too coherent, because while the answer is complex, the "news" that emerges from the conversation is as follows: *Strong Towns believes your suburban house will soon be sold as salvage material.*

Oh yes, that is a great way to win friends and influence people, is it not?

If you've not read the report, let me give you the elevator speech: The American pattern of suburban development is a huge social experiment begun after World War II. To the extent that it has been "successful", that success has been predicated on a series of one-time events such as

America's primacy in the world of finance, abundant cheap energy and the underlying financial mechanisms of the suburban development pattern itself. In pursuit of prosperity, we've over invested in infrastructure that is simply not productive enough to be sustained. This reality is forcing a change in how we grow and develop our cities, towns and neighborhoods.

So what will happen to all this stuff we have built that we can't afford to maintain? The simple answer is that, if we can't afford to maintain it, we won't. Stuff will start to fail and, initially, will be patched together. We're already in this phase, actually. When resources get tight enough, things will fail and they will not be restored. We'll simply accept that failure and it will become the new normal.

There is a precedent for this in American history, albeit one much different from this situation. At the beginning of the Suburban Experiment, we largely abandoned our central cities. Resources, while not scarce at that time, were diverted away from the maturing of our core cities and into suburban development. What you saw in these cities was a general decline that became normal. In fact, for those born and raised outside of an urban area (myself being one), the decline and decay of the urban core has been the prevailing narrative of big cities until recently.

Suburban decline is going to be vastly different and far messier than the urban decline of two generations ago. First, it is not going to involve a diversion of resources but a lack of resources. This has huge implications, especially when one ponders the demographic makeup of much of suburbia. Second, despite an individual's affection for their own sheetrock palace, very little of suburbia is "loveable" (to steal a term from the great Steve Mouzon and The Original Green[xxxix]). We are going to have difficulties acting collectively in its defense. Third and most important, the lack of productivity of suburban development is our underlying economic problem -- the weight on our backs, so to speak -- and as soon as that is fully understood by the electorate (and we're getting closer) there is not going to be a lot of desire to take collective money to prop up the suburban lifestyle.

For these reasons and more, I see four potential fates for those homes and businesses that currently exist throughout suburban America.

1. Lower Entropy. I think many of these places can persist, albeit at a lower state of existence. My sense (or my hope) is that the home I live in falls into this category. There will be fewer trips to town -- more by bicycle and fewer by car -- and we'll rely more on our garden and the lakes and forests around us for our living. This is not unlike the conditions I grew up in on the farm a few miles from here. We were quite isolated, despite being only a short distance from town. It should be understood that the roads were very "rural"; low speed and low volume. Nothing like we have today. I sense they will devolve back in that direction rather precipitously. A trip to town was a big deal when I was growing up. It will be again.

2. Neighborhood Repair. Some of the suburban subdivisions can recreate themselves into something that could be viable in a New Economy. There are some really intelligent people working on this over at the Incremental Sprawl Repair Working Group[xl] and the work of Galina Tachieva and her Sprawl Repair Manual is nothing short of brilliant[xli]. Obviously, the prevailing densities suggest that the further you go out from the urban core and the closer you get to exurban areas, the more difficult this strategy will be.

3. Abandonment. I toured a gorgeous building in downtown St. Paul last spring that had been abandoned decades ago. As my friend described it; *"It was as if the shift got over, everyone got up from their sewing machines, walked out the door and never came back."* As property values continue to decline along with the demand for suburban, commuter-driven living, we're certain to see the same abandonment of suburban buildings. In fact, there are many that are abandoned today, vacant except for a "for sale" sign (or foreclosure notice) that has been in place for years.

4. Salvage. This is the most controversial outcome (and thus widely reported) but there is ample proof in the common episodes of copper thievery that salvageable parts of suburban homes will be reused. Back in the early days of the United States when nails were very rare and expensive, it was not uncommon for a home to be burnt to the ground as a way to salvage the nails. When the individual components of a building have a higher total value than the assembled structure, the market will turn that structure into salvage. Note that global competition for commodities such as copper, iron and timber and even for things like appliances and fixtures will continue to drive up their individual value even as the overall value of the suburban home declines for an entirely different set of reasons.

Nobody wants to be told that the highest and best use of their house is for salvage. I sit at my kitchen table right now in a house that I built myself and I have a hard time imagining someone in here removing the trim, pulling out the windows, ripping up the floor and taking out the wiring that I so painstakingly put together. The pictures of my kids are on the walls and my dog is sleeping in the spot where we always put the Christmas tree! I can't even imagine moving just those things, let alone salvaging the building materials from the house.

But what happens when the city no longer maintains the road in front of my house? What happens when the county can't afford to maintain the six miles of overbuilt road that gets me to the highway? What happens when that highway is no longer maintained, or at least has only minimal maintenance? What happens when gasoline is $5 per gallon? $8 per gallon? $15 per gallon? What happens when my few neighbors are forced to abandon their homes? What happens when the police and fire departments are no longer able to serve us this remotely?

I suspect that things will change. My greatest hope is that our local leaders will get out in front of this and adapt their approach to the new realities. The other option -- denial of the seriousness of problem until the system collapses -- is what we seem to be headed for right now in the financial markets of Europe. This appears to be the default setting for humanity.

Are we any different? I'm optimistic, but only because there are so many people that want things to change. Americans want to live in Strong Towns. Actually, that too is humanity's default setting.

WHY I BECAME A NEW URBANIST

(May 23, 2011) The 19th Congress for the New Urbanism kicks off next week in Madison, Wisconsin. While the New Urbanist movement was founded by architects, it has expanded far beyond that base and into nearly every profession that touches on the way we build or inhabit places. I've personally come to view New Urbanism as the best model to describe prosperous human habitat. It has continued to be the answer to all of the critical questions I have asked myself throughout my professional career.

I just spent two and a half days in Orlando, Florida, at a conference on Economic Gardening. I stayed in a hotel at Disneyworld and had the opportunity to spend a few hours at the Magic Kingdom, the theme park modeled on California's Disneyland. This is where my journey to New Urbanism began nearly three decades ago.

That may appall some traditional New Urbanists and other design-types that find all things Disney to be some type of placemaking con job. Fake fronts and hyper-reality. Well, if that is your opinion, so be it. You can call the Magic Kingdom my gateway drug if you would like, but what it did was open my eyes to the difference that design makes.

As a young boy, I traveled in the back of a station wagon from our farm in rural Minnesota across the country to Orlando. My family and I had no real idea what we were about to see as none of us had ever been to Disneyworld. I was in awe by the place. Yes, the rides were fantastic and good fun, but the place just blew me away. My prior experience with parks was the county fair - dirty, smelly, muddy and a little seedy. At Disney there didn't seem to be even a blade of grass out of place.

And then there were the lights. That was the moment I clearly remember as hooking me in. During the parade we were sitting down in Frontierland and I watched the special spotlights used for the parade automatically rise up from behind the facade of the building. I understood right there -- even as an adolescent -- that the people who had designed this place knew that a set of spotlights did not belong on the top of a building from the frontier age. They hid them and then, when everyone's attention was diverted to the parade, secretly lifted them up. When the parade was over I watched and, sure enough, they went away. I felt I was in on a deep Disney secret, and my love of such design details has only grown.

It was at Fort Dix New Jersey, sweating away the summer "vacation" between my junior and senior year of high school in Army Basic Training, that I decided I wanted to be a civil engineer. I was good at math, enjoyed science and while my second love was music, my first was my girlfriend (now my wife) and I did not think I could be a decent future husband on a musician's salary (you don't join the Army at age 17 unless you are either thinking ahead or not thinking at all). Civil engineering was an opportunity for me to "build cities", which is what my placemaking obsession had evolved to by that point.

And that I did. When I graduated, I got a job in my hometown and started building cities. Or at least parts of cities; largely it was new subdivisions. I did the occasional municipal sewer and water project and even did an airport expansion. It was challenging work and I liked it a lot. But there was something I was looking for that was missing.

This is about the time that I first heard of the New Urbanism, and it came from the Disney Company's development of the town of Celebration.[xlii] I was absolutely enthralled by it. The layout, the design, the architecture and, of course, the front porches. I had already built my own house -- complete with a front porch -- but I yearned to live in a place like Celebration, which was different in a way I could not quite explain. Since they would not send marketing information to Minnesota, I had my best friend, Mike Tester, who was living in Texas at the time, order it for me. I still have it.

About this time I was being encouraged to go back to graduate school. I had reached a professional plateau at work and my mentor, George Orning, was suggesting the answers to the questions he had been helping to plant in my head may be found at the Humphrey Institute and their Masters of Urban and Regional Planning program.

Here was my second bite at the New Urbanism apple and I'll never forget this moment in my first week there. The professor was talking about transit systems (a foreign concept to me at that point) and casually threw out a question on which type of street network functioned better, grid or curvilinear. The answer was obvious to me as I had just spent six years designing and building curvilinear streets and, of course, I would only have done that if they were the best. As my eager hand went up someone said, "*uh...grid*" in a voice that sounded like "*uh...duh*" and, before my hand even went down, the professor said, "*of course*," then went on with the lecture as if such an obvious point was not even worth making.

Graduate school continued to expose me to the planning concepts surrounding New Urbanism. I found that it was more than just front porches and pleasant places, it actually had functional advantages that the subdivisions from the standard zoning manual did not have. People didn't have to drive everywhere. Neighborhoods could be reclaimed. Housing could be affordable. But I was a long ways gone and so it took a couple more bites at the apple for me to come around completely.

During graduate school I formed my own planning organization, Community Growth Institute, where I still work today. My modest mission for CGI was to "*Save Rural America*", which earned me a few giggles from my peers but, fortunately, a few contracts as well. We did a lot of zoning work originally -- kind of like an outsourced zoning department for small towns -- and my thought was that, if I could just put really smart people into these places, I could help them do a lot better.

It was only after years of trying this and failing that I started to see that it was not the people that needed replacing, it was the operating system. Modern zoning was the problem, and it could not be overcome with better educated or more dedicated people. In my search for answers, I attended a conference on the SmartCode in Miami and came face-to-face with more New Urbanism than I could ignore. I met Andres Duany, Steve Mouzon,

Jeff Speck, Hazel Borys, Jennifer Hurley and Nathan Norris, amongst others. I spent my days in awe and my evenings in seclusion trying to process everything I was learning. This SmartCode was definitely part of the answer.[xliii]

But I wasn't a New Urbanist yet. For that I had to make the final, financial connection. One of the things I had grown to understand back in my engineering days was that the finance of our development pattern did not make sense. At first I assumed that it just didn't make sense to me, but that people much smarter or more experienced must know what they were doing. As I met these people, I realized that they were really not all that smart. In fact, many were complete idiots.

As the design and regulatory questions subsided, the financial questions began to take more prominence in my life. I began to study finance and put pencil to paper on some of the developments I knew intimately. Then I looked beyond that. What I uncovered was that the underlying finance of our suburban development pattern is a simple Ponzi scheme, one that relies on ever-increasing amounts of new growth to subsidize the existing public liabilities. That truth is the founding revelation for the work I do at Strong Towns.

But if the current approach was destined to bankrupt us, what was a viable alternative? The answer to my question was, once again, the New Urbanism.

I looked back at the way we had built cities here in the United States before the huge federal subsidies for mortgages, interstate highways, local sewer and water systems, oil and gas, agriculture, etc... to see what we did when our places had to actually be financially viable or they went away. What I found was urbanism.

We actually built places that people wanted to live in, not just drive through. We actually built public buildings to create value, not simply function for bureaucrats. We built places that were mixed use in every way, not artificially segmented along socio-economic lines. We accommodated old people without sequestering them into some type of low-security penitentiary setting. We accommodated young people by allowing them a chance to live with other youth, to grow up in the fabric of a community and discover themselves within a society. And we did it all on a framework that we were able to afford to sustain, even as a very poor country of largely uneducated people.

And as I discovered the old urbanism that we had lost, I understood that this was what had been resurrected by the New Urbanists. This was the answer, and it had been in front of me all along.

I still deeply enjoy spending time at Disneyworld and jump at every opportunity I can to go there. I am a hyper-sensory person -- from smell to taste to sound -- and I find it is one of few environments that I feel totally comfortable in. (For example, I was told in a behind-the-scenes tour that every song in the park is in the same key, which explains why the melodies do not contrast as you walk around. This is very comforting to someone like me that can't help but hear every cheesy Barry Manilow organ arrangement piped in as ubiquitous background noise in many retail establishments.) My hope is that, as the practical realities of our financial situation meet our human desires to have lives that are fulfilling, we will find the principles of New Urbanism are not just for theme parks and experimental developments but are actually the DNA of prosperity.

THE DIVERGING DIAMOND

In November of 2010, one of my readers sent me a link to a video promoting a Diverging Diamond Interchange (DDI) in Springfield, MO. The ten minute video was shot from the point of view of an enthusiastic man walking through the DDI, holding a video camera and providing a running narrative. He was very proud of all of the great features contained in the interchange, particularly those that made the improvement "pedestrian friendly".

This all struck me as rather bizarre. While on paper, the DDI may have met all of the checklist items for pedestrians, the video itself showed a place that was auto dominated and despotic. The fact that the narrator believed what he was saying – that the red brick used in the islands made it "nice" or that the center trench provided pedestrians with a "beautiful view" of the interstate – only made it all seem more surreal.

In the office I shared the video with my colleagues and, during the part where the narrator walks through the center trench, I played the Imperial Theme from the Star Wars series. We were all in stitches and soon I was compelled to put together my own video narration. I not only wanted to have some fun but to demonstrate just how messed up our thinking currently is and how far we need to go to actually build places that have value.

While there was generally a positive reaction from those who follow my work, there was a very strong negative reaction from a number of places.

People supported the DDI for being more affordable and a better use of infrastructure (something I constantly advocate for), felt it gave pedestrians something where before they had nothing and thought I was unrealistic in comparing this interchange to scenes in England or Holland where there is a different culture for pedestrians and bikers.

In the following essays I go through and address those critiques.

Dear Engineers

(November 10, 2011) I want to highlight a couple of intelligent criticisms of my Diverging Diamond video critique.

The first criticism is essentially an argument of context; I've gotten the context wrong and am way off base if I have an expectation that this highway interchange should be like a pedestrian street in the U.K. or Holland. Here are some of those comments collected from various sources:

> *"Sorry to state the obvious, but this is a freeway interchange. Designing it to be a pleasant beautiful place to be is about as absurd as expecting a lakefront promenade to move cars at 60 mph."*

* * * * *

> *"This rebuttal reflects a serious lack of context on Marohn's part. This intersection *is* the intersection of a busy local road and an interstate highway. It is not central Amsterdam. It is not a residential part of Portland. It is the kind of place where there is an expressway, a few gas stations, and maybe a Cracker Barrel. The first three points were to move cars because that is the essence of that intersection. The more realistic criticism would be that they bothered to do anything for bikes and pedestrians. I'm guessing both are pretty rare there."*

* * * * *

> *"Why are you comparing a freeway interchange in the outskirts of Springfield, Missouri to bikeways in central Amsterdam or streets in☐ urban UK? A fairer comparison would be with an interchange under a similar setting in Europe, the US, or elsewhere."*

* * * * *

"Complaining that foot traffic has to navigate a potentially snow-covered ditch seriously misses the point - if this were someplace where people actually needed to reach and cross the intersection on foot, there'd be sidewalks."

The second criticism of my critique is a lesser-of-all-evils argument; you think this is bad, you should see what it could have been. Some of those comments:

"Er...you do know this was the best the could retrofit onto the existing bridge, right? It's not a "complete streets" solution by any stretch of the imagination and it shouldn't be viewed that way. On the ones I've worked on, the center channel (and that is the best place to put it) is at least 14' wide. The right shoulder in both directions should be between 8-10' wide and striped as a bike lane. The cross section on this project reflects only what they could fit on the existing bridge. When you account for the fact that they added about 35% more capacity at a low cost and little in the way of new pavement and no work on the bridge, it's pretty remarkable. It was a functional decision. And it's leaps and bounds better for bikes and peds than it was before."

* * * * *

"Criticizing an interstate highway interchange on the far northern outskirts of a small mid-western city for not looking like central London or Amsterdam seems excessively snobby and snarky. Short of dynamiting one of the two interstate highways through Missouri, I'm not sure how Marohn could have done a better job designing the interchange to be bike and pedestrian friendly."

In response, my good friend and colleague, Nate Hood[xliv], provided these thoughts:

"At the heart of it, I think Marohn is trying to touch on two separate issues: 1) "Checklist planning," which is to say that developers will add sidewalks or bike paths to hit the ADA and/or Zoning requirement without even considering how it relates to its surrounding environment. And, 2) Community Investments: While it might not be fair to compare suburban Springfield, MO to Amsterdam, it shows us the stark contrast of how we've decided to spend money and invest in our own communities in the United States versus how other places in the world have decided to invest their limited capital resources."

I'll add to Nate's brilliant comment by noting the following:

If you watch the original video that my comments were based off of, the gentlemen giving the tour was touting how pedestrian- and cycling- friendly this interchange was. That is absurd. This interchange is not "friendly" to pedestrians or cyclists. Suggestions that red decorative brick or yellow markings on the sidewalks would make it so are absurd.

If we in the engineering profession can't step back and acknowledge the absurdity of this situation -- the absurdity that mindless adherence to standards has created -- how can we expect to be taken seriously as leaders by a country going through a difficult and painful economic transition?

It is not good enough to simply follow the American Society of Civil Engineers and the Infrastructure Cult and demand ever more money for our profession when we turn around and waste it in spectacular amounts on things that provide no return (in this instance, moving cars a little faster and building expensive pedestrian/bike facilities that will never be widely used because they are despotic and demeaning). If we engineers want to be part of the solution, we need to reorient ourselves away from our obsession with moving cars more efficiently and towards building places of value.

Getting cars from the Quiki-Mart to the Wal-Mart in 45 seconds instead of 60 seconds is not a good enough contribution to society to justify the money our profession is spending. We are fooling ourselves by pretending we are being "innovative" just because we add red brick, some sidewalk treatments and a cycling trench. Realizing that many are acting in this way in response to financial incentive programs that reward "complete streets" designs only adds to my disgust.

The United States needs great engineers. When are we going to stop being mindless technocrats and go back to being a real profession?

A 45 MPH World

(November 21, 2011) We've built a 45 mile per hour world, one that moves too slowly to be efficient yet too fast to provide a platform for value. Our transportation system embraces mediocrity, not from a lack of resources, but from a lack of focus. We must quit fooling ourselves, understand what it means to really create value in a transportation system and commit ourselves to building Strong Towns.

It seems like I've offended everyone at least a little bit with my commentary questioning the pedestrian friendliness of the Diverging Diamond Interchange (or DDI for short, as I've found out they call it *in the biz*). I'll take one comment from @cartographer1977 as representative of the criticism I think most important to address:

> *"The problem is not the concept of the DDI but rather the poor pedestrian and bicycle facilities at this particular DDI".*

The Diverging Diamond Interchange may be a fantastic way to move more auto traffic in less time and with more safety than using a standard interchange. One could also argue that the modest pedestrian facilities -- ridiculous afterthought though they may be -- are a step in the right direction, acknowledgment of the need to safely accommodate the long-neglected non-auto traffic.

The problem with these observations is that they are rooted in a fantasy world, one we've created for ourselves, complete with false metrics and all the confirmation bias necessary to avoid reality. It is tough to have an intelligent discussion on the DDI because, in order to do so, we need to step way, way back and truly understand our transportation system.

Let me start by pointing out one cold, hard fact: **We do not have anywhere near the money necessary to maintain our current surface transportation system.**

The Federal Highway Trust Fund[xlv] is broke. Projections give it dimes on the dollar of what is necessary to maintain the systems we have created. Those problems simply roll downhill, and so our states are in a position just as difficult, if not more so. States, not having the revenues to maintain their systems or the ability to raise more revenue, have turned to debt to forestall the day of reckoning. Just look at Texas -- allegedly one of the country's most prosperous, as well as auto-obsessed, states -- and see how they have used debt to kick the can down the road.

> *"As governor, Perry advocated the controversial Trans-Texas Corridor, an ambitious transportation scheme that relied on foreign investment and tolls for financing. It was abandoned after the outcry from property owners whose land would have been claimed by eminent domain.*
>
> *Since then, the state has relied heavily on issuance of bonds to build highways. For the first time in history, the Texas Legislature this year appropriated more cash to pay for debt service than to pay for actually building new roads: $850 million per year versus $575 million.*
>
> *Lawmakers also approved the use of $3 billion approved by voters in 2007 for road construction, but the Texas Department of Transportation estimates the state must pay $65 million in annual financing costs for every $1 billion it borrows through the sale of bonds.*
>
> *The state began borrowing money in 2003 to pay for roads and will owe $17.3 billion by the end of next year, contributing to the rapid escalation of total state debt, from $13.4 billion in 2001 to $37.8 billion today.*
>
> *The money will cover just a fraction of the transportation needs identified by planning experts. The Texas Transportation Institute two years ago placed the state's highway construction needs through 2030 at $488 billion."[xlvi]*

The second fact that needs to be acknowledged is this: **The system we've built is financially inefficient and unproductive.**

This is where I'm going to lose a lot of engineers who believe that each part of *"The System"* can be inefficient and dumb yet, somehow magically when combined, *"The System"* overall becomes this awesome engine of American prosperity. This is the fantasy part I referred to earlier. What gives us this belief?

It can't be the numbers. I reported earlier this year how the American Society of Civil Engineers' own report showed that the costs to maintain the current surface transportation system at *"minimum tolerable conditions"* far exceed any of the benefits, even as they massively inflated the benefits.

And do we really believe, as just one example of many, that saving a few thousand cars from having to sit at a railroad crossing each day translates into $47 million worth of wealth created?[xlvii] We deliver ourselves a derivation of this lie every time we make a major transportation investment.

But go beyond the numbers. We build an interchange on a highway -- diamond or otherwise -- and what happens? We get a Wal-Mart, a couple of gas stations and a Pet Smart. Does anyone believe for a second that, without this investment, people wouldn't find a way to buy cheap imported goods, gasoline and dog food? The United States has six times the retail space per capita of any European country.[xlviii] There are diminishing returns here. We're long past anything that makes economic sense in a true market economy.

Go ahead and argue that if we simply paid more in taxes we could afford our surface transportation system. That is ASCE's argument -- we're a wealthy country, after all. Well, besides the fact that you would be living in a fantasy world (because it's not going to happen), it wouldn't help if it did.

Raise the gas tax enough to make a difference (we're talking $2 or $3 per gallon in my home state of Minnesota, according to people I've spoken with at MnDOT who have done the calculations). What would happen? People would drive a lot, lot less. We would then have the money to maintain a bunch a roads that people wouldn't be using -- not a viable long-term policy. Okay, how about switch to a mileage tax. Again, when you charge people by the mile you'll find that people will avoid paying the charge by reducing their trips, at least if the charge is anywhere near high enough to reflect the cost. Maybe you think people driving less is a great solution, but if you do, you can't be arguing that our money currently is well spent by expanding the capacities of "*The System*".

So maybe we should just take money from the general fund (incidentally, this is what we have been doing). In that case, there would continue to be no connection between what people want (more capacity) and what people are willing to pay (little to nothing) and we go right on building more in the current, unproductive model. The lack of productivity -- the lack of an ability to capture any financial return -- would ultimately catch up to us again (as it has now) and we're right back to where we started, only with even more of "*The System*" to maintain.

This leads to the third fact about our surface transportation system: **Americans do not understand the difference between a road and a street.**[xlix]

Roads move people between places while streets provide a framework for capturing value within a place.

The value of a road is in the speed and efficiency that it provides for movement between places. Anything that is done that reduces the speed and efficiency of a road devalues that road. If we want to maximize the value of a road, we eliminate anything that reduces the speed and efficiency of travel.

The value of a street comes from its ability to support land use patterns that create a financial return. The street with the highest value is the one that creates the greatest amount of tax revenue with the least amount of public expense over multiple life cycles. If we want to maximize the value of a street, we design it in such a way that it supports an adjacent development pattern that is financially resilient, architecturally timeless and socially enduring.

These simple concepts are totally lost on us, especially those in the engineering profession. If you want to start to see the world with Strong Towns eyes and truly understand why our development approach is bankrupting us, just watch your speedometer. Anytime you are traveling between 30 and 50 miles per hour, you are basically in an area that is too slow to be efficient yet too fast to provide a framework for capturing a productive rate of return.

In the United States, we've built a 45 mile per hour world for ourselves. It is truly the worst of all possible approaches. Our neighborhoods are filled with STROADS (street/road hybrids) that spread investment out horizontally, making it extremely difficult to capture the amount of value necessary for the public to sustain the transportation systems that serve them. Between our neighborhoods, towns and cities we have built STROADS that are encumbered with intersections, vehicles turning across traffic, merging cars and people taking routine local trips. These are not fast, safe and efficient corridors.

At best, the Diverging Diamond Interchange is putting lipstick on a pig. At worst, it is a continuation of our delusional fantasy that somehow we can sustain prosperity without building places of value. The Death Star pedestrian trench is despotic and demeaning. In the big picture, it is also an utterly meaningless waste of money.

We need to build places of value. We need to start building Strong Towns.

Understanding Roads

(November 29, 2011) Americans are spending immense sums of money making cosmetic improvements to a transportation system that is simply not working. Traffic engineers, lacking the correct tools to actually solve traffic problems, have convinced themselves that they are fighting the good fight. They are supported by local government officials, anxious for that next hit of growth that will give the local economy a temporary high. It is a destructive alliance, one that we can no longer afford.

I don't want to pick on Springfield, MO. I have to admit that I've never been there, but I do like Missouri in general and have enjoyed my time there (except that summer at Fort Leonardwood -- yuck, I hate clay and chiggers). I'm sure Springfield is a great place filled with great people. They just have the poor fortune of having had a local booster make a ridiculous video touting the "pedestrian-friendly features" of their diverging diamond interchange and, well.... It's not personal, Springfield.

To understand the problems we face, we need to examine the so-called roads feeding into the interchange. That would be Missouri 13, supposedly a highway of some sort. Missouri state statutes define a highway rather broadly in Section 300.010, actually indicating that a "street" is the same as a "highway":

> *"Street" or "highway", the entire width between the lines of every way publicly maintained when any part thereof is open to the uses of the public for purposes of vehicular travel. "State highway", a highway maintained by the state of Missouri as a part of the state highway system;[1]*

Maybe they mean that it could be a street OR a highway if it is publicly maintained and used for vehicular travel. It makes little difference, as we will see, because they've actually built neither a street nor a highway.

The photo below (credit: Google Earth) shows the diverging diamond and the surrounding land use. Notice that Missouri 13 (which runs north/south) intersects Missouri Route 744 about half a mile south of the diverging diamond. This is the short stretch of STROAD (street/road hybrid) we're going to focus on.

The Missouri DOT, using $3 million of state and federal funds, built the DDI. It was reported at the time that a regular interchange would have cost $10 million, making the DDI not only safer but much cheaper. This is the core of the argument in favor of the DDI, which I really don't disagree with. If you diagnose the problem here as one of traffic, then by all means, use the cheaper and safer alternative. And that is how they diagnosed it: "tremendous traffic problems".

"Don Saiko, PE, who is a project manager in the Springfield, Missouri District of MODOT, got word of the DDI concept and wanted to investigate the design in the Springfield area. He got permission to test the design at I-44 and Kansas Expressway (SR 13) which had

been experiencing tremendous traffic problems and safety issues due mainly to the small left turn storage areas to the ramps. A $10 million budget was given for the construction of this project. The simulations for the design looked very promising to fix the traffic and safety problems. It was also a very cost effective solution. The DDI was only going to cost about $3 million, saving the state $7 million of the budgeted cost, which would have been the cost for a conventional diamond solution. [ii]

If you only have a hammer, every problem becomes a nail, even if your hammer is a European import.

Unfortunately, like all DOT's that I have ever studied or interacted with, the problem in this situation was misdiagnosed. It was not traffic -- or more specifically the stacking and congestion of traffic -- at the interchange. The problem is how the public's investment in Missouri 13 has been debased for short-term economic gain and how, in the process, the corridor has been made unworkable as an actual highway.

Here's what I'm talking about. In order to support the adjacent land use that you see in the picture above, that single half mile of Missouri 13 -- a state **HIGHWAY** -- contains 29 intersections (each marked with an 'X' in the photo below). That is an intersection roughly every 100 feet. You can't have a highway with smooth, free-flowing, efficient traffic patterns when you also try and accommodate that type of land use pattern.

And look at some of these intersections up close. It is just plain bizarre, especially for a supposedly high-capacity roadway, one I'm certain we've invested millions of federal dollars to build and maintain.

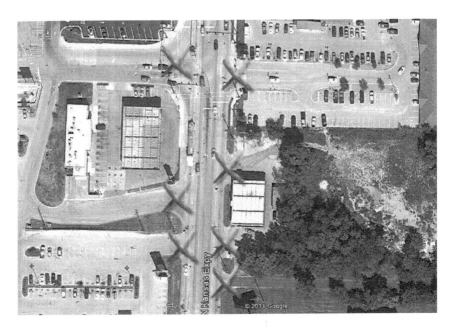

Who are these engineers kidding? What type of improved traffic flow do they really think they are creating by spending $3 million up the street on an interchange? What type of safety improvements do they think they are making at an interchange when they have vastly more dangerous STROAD built like this?

This reminds me of the New Testament parable about looking at the sliver in your neighbor's eye while ignoring the beam in your own. Are we honestly looking at this corridor and diagnosing the traffic problem here as the interchange? Or is it just that the transportation funding -- not to mention the short term local land use incentives -- favor dealing with slivers and not beams?

And this is just one half mile. This pattern extends a long ways along Ol' Missouri 13.

This is far from an efficient transportation system. If you give me $10 million to spend here, I spend it closing accesses. You can do more to improve traffic flow and efficiency by closing these accesses than anything else. All you have here is a bunch of people making inefficient local trips on a highway sized for high-speed, through traffic. That's not a traffic problem. It's a land use problem.

Of course, we can't close accesses. In the United States, people who own land adjacent to highways have a God-given right to highway access, regardless of the impact. And when an access is taken away, they must be compensated (although it should be noted, when the highway was built, is improved or their access is enhanced, that is just the public's responsibility and by no means should that cost be assessed to them). It is the local land use version of *"heads I win, tails you lose"* because -- in our current system -- the public is either forced to invest endlessly in a transportation approach that can never truly work or are going to pay huge sums of money in compensation.

If those are the only two choices we have, I refuse to play the game. I would not spend another dime on this waste of a corridor.

Let me finish by making two related observations. The major impetus for building the DDI here was supposedly safety, as it supposedly is in all similar transportation "enhancements" (see earlier conversation on slivers and beams). In fact, I had to laugh at a AAA spokesman who bought into this racket:

> *"Mike Right, spokesman for AAA Missouri, said the new design is a positive change, as it reduces construction costs while moving traffic faster and more safely. As motorists have adjusted to roundabouts, American drivers will learn and adapt to the diverging diamond, he said."[lii]*

I'm assuming that he drove the Missouri 13 STROAD -- about the least safe traffic environment you could be in, with high-speed designs mashed up with turning traffic, stop and go traffic, sudden lane changes and obnoxious signage -- thinking that was just fine.

Which leads me to my other observation: Is this all worth it? Yeah, you got the Wal-Mart investment there, but really, does anyone in Springfield believe this is more than a near-term benefit? If you do think this is a great long-term investment, I have a challenge for you. Drive south along Missouri 13 until you find the area that was built 30 years ago. How's that area looking? How's it holding up?

I'm going to venture an educated guess that it's not. Like the land use around the DDI intersection, it was designed for one life cycle. It will not retain its value, it will not be adequately maintained. Within our Suburban Experiment, today's new thing is tomorrow's place in decline and the future's slum. For some reason we accept that in America. We need to step back and realize that, in the course of human history, it is not normal. Or healthy. Or financially viable.

The time to start building Strong Towns is now.

What now, Chuck?

(November 30, 2011) People are always looking for simple solutions. I'm routinely asked give city officials the one or two things that should be done to fix their current economic problems. Those things don't exist. If there were a painless, simple way to solve our problems, we certainly would have done it. In fact, part of the reason we are here today is that we've done the simple and relatively painless thing for so long. The following are some more effective, options.

The common frustration with my analysis of the Springfield, MO, diverging diamond investment and the surrounding land use pattern is summarized in this comment I received after the initial article was published:

> *"I agree 100% that this area is poorly designed, pedestrian-hostile, and dangerous; that Walmart is a cancer on the economy and on society; and that were we to start from scratch this outcome ought to be considered a monstrous failure. But here in the real world, we have a busy and dangerous street, a bottleneck overpass to an area where a lot of commuters live, hundreds of millions of dollars worth of existing infrastructure in place. Do you leave the area to rot? If not, how do you improve it?"*

Ah, the "*real world*". I respect the point, of course, but also get frustrated by the limitations we put on ourselves. So much of our dysfunction is simple inertia. Changing our approach is so difficult. We know, for instance, that something like Medicare spending is unsustainable, but we also realize that collectively we are unlikely to do anything substantive to deal with the problem until we're actually in a crisis. Some of that is human nature. Some of it is the variant of democracy that we have evolved into.

In a prior essay I gave three critical insights for understanding my critique of this investment. They are:

1. We don't have anywhere near the money necessary to maintain our

current surface transportation system.

2. The system we've built is financially inefficient and unproductive.

3. Americans do not understand the difference between a road and a street.

On the first point specifically, the crisis is coming. It is actually already here, but we've been using debt to put off the reckoning a little while longer. We don't have nearly enough money to maintain all of the systems we've built. (Note that you can argue that we do have the money, and technically you would be right, but it is the same as arguing that someone should be able to pay their $2,000 monthly mortgage on an annual salary of $30,000. Technically they could, but in the real world, they can't.) Since each increment of investment in the current system makes us financially weaker over the long-term, our approach is ultimately going to force a crisis. In short, at some point very soon we're going to look at the *"real world"* in a very different way.

Here are two simple ideas of mine that would effectively deal with the STROAD (street/road hybrid) problem within a generation.

Idea #1: End the State Aid System

Each state has its own version of a state aid program. I'll focus on Minnesota's with the informed belief that other states are similar in their approach.

The Minnesota non-profit Fresh Energy explains how money is allocated between the highway system and the local state aid system.

> *"Dedicated state funding (the money that comes from the gas tax, tab fees, and the motor vehicle sales tax) is allocated by formula through something called the Highway User Tax Distribution Fund. The State Trunk Highway Fund receives 62 percent to build and maintain Mn/DOT highways, the County State Aid Fund receives 29 percent to pay for county roads, the Municipal State Aid Fund gets 9 percent to take care of roads in cities, and 5 percent is set aside for purposes determined by the Legislature. Most of the federal money comes through formulas as well, while it is predominately targeted toward the state highway system. Between 2004 and 2008, an average of 84 percent of federal money went to the state highways while cities,*

In short, large sums of money are collected at the state and federal levels for transportation and then a portion of that money is transferred back to local governments for transportation. Along with the money come requirements that dictate how it is to be used. These include engineering requirements for things such as lane width, degree of road curvature and design speed and planning requirements for things like maintaining a hierarchical road network.

In the "*real world*", the state aid system is the primary funding mechanism for the worst design practices at the local level. Most STROADS are built using this funding. Financially, these are the least productive of all transportation investments, spending enormous sums of money to speed up purely local trips by nominal amounts of time. These STROADS are often constructed right through the middle of existing neighborhoods, lowering their value in the process.

Let me provide three local examples so you can start to see these places in your community (they are everywhere).

(1) When I was a kid riding the bus we used to travel down Knollwood Drive in Baxter. It was a local street that ran through a post-WW II subdivision, with lake-fronting properties on one side and off-lake on the other, curving streets and a lot of cul-de-sacs. This was an early suburban-era design -- I would guess 1960's -- and so, even in my youth, the infrastructure was showing its age. It was a bumpy bus ride.

Sometime in the mid-1990's, the city of Baxter reached population levels where they qualified for state aid transportation funding. State aid rules require the designation of state aid routes, corridors that begin and end on state highways or other state-funded corridors. Knollwood fit the bill and so a convenient remedy to repair the failing infrastructure along Knollwood was to designate it a state aid route.

Of course the residents did not like this one bit. This was a small neighborhood, not a major transportation corridor. But as the project proceeded and was combined with sewer and water extensions as well as other "improvements", the price tag climbed to levels where accepting the state aid designation, along with the significant money, was the lesser of two evils.

In the photo below I've highlighted Knollwood. You can clearly see that it serves no significant purpose in terms of regional transportation. At best it is a shortcut through an otherwise-sleepy neighborhood, allowing someone to save a few seconds or a minute on getting from one place to another.

(2) The city of East Gull Lake has a small dam that serves as the crossing of the Gull River. It is a single lane crossing and so you have to stop on each end and then yield to oncoming traffic. It is actually kind of charming and, particularly in the middle of a campground/recreation area, does a lot to calm traffic.

Unfortunately, the approach to the dam from the west is a county state aid road (CSAH 70) while the approach from the east is a simple county road (CR 125), a road not supported with state aid money. The catch here is that CR 125 was decrepit and in need of maintenance. The cost was (and the exact figures allude me so I'm going on memory) somewhere around $1.2 million. Because CR 125 was not a state aid route, it would be entirely the county's bill.

In order to access state aid money -- along with some other federal grant money -- for this project, the county came up with a plan to connect CSAH 70 with CR 125 using a new bridge across the Gull River. The cost for this project would have been in the many millions of dollars for a new bridge, the widening and realignment of CR 125, the condemnation of a couple of homes, etc... The catch is that the local portion of the project -- the county's share -- would have been only around $600,000 and they could have used state aid money for it.

In retrospect this looks even more ridiculous because, while the bridge project didn't happen and nothing remotely calamitous has transpired from a traffic standpoint since, the public was told at the time that tremendous traffic projections along with safety enhancements made this project a necessity. That was utterly ridiculous. It was simply the ability to access outside funds that pushed the design of the project, not local traffic concerns.

(3) The local heartbreak project in my hometown of Brainerd is College Drive, which I call *My Hometown's Last Great Old Economy project*. I've written extensively about this project in the past because it is a perfect example of the destruction wrought by the state aid system. Poor neighborhood in decline on one side, local community college on the other side. Instead of building a sensible project that would connect the two and strengthen each (local cost around $1.2 million), we instead leverage our next four years' worth of state aid dollars, along with other federal "stimulus" money, to build a $9 million, 4-lane STROAD. Local cost for the STROAD is less than $1 million.

The state aid system actually makes it cheaper for the city to build a destructive corridor -- one whose central outcome will be to allow the people of South Brainerd to reach the Wal-Mart in neighboring Baxter 45 seconds more quickly -- than to build a neighborhood-affirming corridor, one that would capitalize on all of the existing investments made by the city and its residents in this area.

Ending the state aid system -- eliminating the funding of local auto-based transportation along with the planning and design mandates that accompany it -- would effectively end the destructive practice of building terrible local transportation corridors. And it would accomplish this within a generation. As soon as these corridors became decrepit, local values and sensibilities would demand that their replacement respond to the community, not outside design criteria.

Note that I am not arguing that the there should be no role for the state in funding local transportation. That is a completely different discussion. All I'm arguing is that the state aid system is broken and should not be "reformed" but should simply go away.

Idea #2: Institute an Accessibility Tax

There is talk about funding transportation improvements through an increase in the gas tax, a mileage tax, tolls roads, increased allocations of general fund revenues, etc... Each of these has upsides and downsides, but none of them do anything to address the fundamental lack of productivity inherent in the current system. They would all simply be new revenue streams that would reinforce the unsustainable status quo for a little while longer.

One of the problems we run up against in building quality roads is that it is really difficult to close accesses. There are all kinds of constitutional issues around takings that make it very difficult and costly. I don't want to have that argument -- heads you win, tails I lose -- regarding the cost and benefits of improving a transportation corridor when you don't have any control over the access. Let's allow as much access as there is demand, but let's charge for it.

There are no constitutional issues for a state when it comes to taxing or tolling on roads. We should institute an access tax (or toll) that would be designed to, in a sense, compensate the public for the decrease in capacity caused by the access. It would work something like this.

On a rural country road where you have 1,000 cars a day, putting in an access is no big deal. You have a driveway that goes out to the highway and it is no problem to wait for the car that may be happening to drive by when you pull out. Your driveway, and the turning movements it creates, does not inhibit the flow of traffic on that corridor in any way. Your tax would be very low, perhaps $20 per year.

On a very busy highway, something with say 20,000 cars per day, Wal-Mart would like to build a new store. They want a traffic signal and a 3/4 interchange on the north and south ends of their property, respectively. Okay, we know from the math used to justify highway projects how much cost adding those accesses would create for the public. It is the opposite of the "benefit" improved mobility would create. Here's how the math would work.[liv]

Let's say the new signal and intersection delayed the average car by one minute. At 20,000 cars per day, one minute each, in a year you have a total delay of 122,000 hours. If we hold to the belief expressed in so many reports justifying highway expansions that this time should be valued at (on the low end) $13.40 per hour, then that signal has a cost to society of $1.6 million per year.

If Wal-Mart wants that signal -- if the local unit of government wants that access -- than there should be a tax/toll/charge of $1.6 million per year to compensate the public for the time lost and the reduction in capacity. That money could be used to enhance the system and restore a comparable amount of mobility elsewhere. I'm not sure who pays it -- the businesses, the drivers or the local unit of government -- but there should be some mechanism for compensation.

(Note that I am proposing this for highways only, not for local streets, the latter of which we need to encourage more access to.)

Such an access tax would not only raise revenue that could be used to improve mobility, it would have two other immediate impacts. First, property owners eager to avoid the access tax would immediately and voluntarily start closing accesses along major highway corridors. Not only would this improve traffic flow and mobility, it would dramatically improve safety. The more the traffic along the corridor, the more incentive to squeeze more value out of it or close it.

Second, and most important, it would actually restore the local property market to something based on place and not something based on government transportation decisions. Decisions on land use would again be local. With local decision-making, where the financial costs and benefits are also local, there would be strong incentives to, once again, start building places of value. We would immediately get away from the too-big-to-fail mega subdivisions on the edge of town and again start incrementally wringing value out of our places, block by block, neighborhood by neighborhood.

Where an additional access to the highway was needed, there would be every incentive to maximize the value capture from that access. You wouldn't have a traffic signal that you have to sit at where there is simply a gas station, a donut shop and some storage sheds. That type of land use would not be viable, not because of the tax but because it actually is not viable without the enormous transportation subsidy we currently provide. Our highways could not only function as highways (fast, efficient connections between places), but our places would start to redefine themselves along a financially-sustainable pattern. They would have to or they would fail.

Now there's the catch, and so I'm not pretending this proposal would be easy to get passed or easy to implement. It would, by ending the perverse transportation subsidy we've created, expose all of the poorly- and inefficiently- configured spaces that we have built in the post-WW II era. That would be extremely painful for many communities. Some would be able, over a generation, to reconfigure themselves in a more viable way. Others would not. Some community triage and support would certainly need to take place. I'm not pretending that I've either the answer for that or have even thought it through enough to suggest how it would happen.

I'll go back to where I started: we don't have the money to maintain everything we've built. Continuing with the status quo approach will only make that problem worse in the long run. We can tinker around the edges with new state aid standards, new federal and state mandates, new taxes and fees, but unless we do something to deal with the core problem -- the financially unproductive nature of the post- WW II land development pattern -- it will not solve the problem.

These two proposals, as difficult as they are to imagine enacting today, would address the real problems we have and do so in a substantive way. While they would certainly create other problems and hardships, doing so is a necessity for getting our places healthy again. We need to think in terms of generations, not months. Phasing in these two approaches over the next few years would set the stage for a renewed Strong Towns discussion in each and every community in America.

And that is something that desperately needs to happen.

THE GROWTH PONZI SCHEME (ABRIDGED)

(June 22, 2011) We often forget that the American's post-WW II approach to development is an experiment, one that has never been tried anywhere before. We assume it is the natural order because it is what we see all around us. But our own history -- let alone a tour of other parts of the world -- suggests a different reality. Across cultures, over thousands of years, people have traditionally built places scaled to the individual. It is only the last two generations that we have scaled places to the automobile.

It is long past time to ask how our experiment is working.

The underlying financing mechanisms of the suburban era – the way we've funded our post-World War II pattern of development -- operates like a classic Ponzi scheme, with ever-increasing rates of growth necessary to sustain long-term liabilities.

Since the end of World War II, our cities and towns have experienced growth using three primary mechanisms[lv]:

(1) Transfer payments between governments: where the federal or state government makes a direct investment in growth at the local level, such as funding a water or sewer system expansion.

(2) Transportation spending: where transportation infrastructure is used to improve access to a site that can then be developed.

(3) Public and private-sector debt: where cities, developers, companies, and

individuals take on debt as part of the development process, whether during construction or through the assumption of a mortgage.

In each of these mechanisms, the local unit of government benefits from the enhanced revenues associated with new growth. It also typically assumes the long-term liability for maintaining the new infrastructure. This exchange -- a near-term cash advantage for a long-term financial obligation -- is one element of a Ponzi scheme.

The other is the realization that the revenue collected does not come near to covering the costs of maintaining the infrastructure. In America, we have a ticking time bomb of unfunded liability for infrastructure maintenance. The American Society of Civil Engineers (ASCE) estimates the cost at $2.2 trillion[lvi] -- but that's just for *major* infrastructure, not the local streets, curbs, walks, and pipes that serve our homes.

The reason we have this gap is because the public yield from the suburban development pattern -- the amount of tax revenue obtained per increment of liability assumed -- is ridiculously low. Over a life cycle, a city frequently receives just a dime or two of revenue for each dollar of liability. The engineering profession will argue, as ASCE does, that we're simply not making the investments necessary to maintain this infrastructure. This is nonsense. We've simply built in a way that is not financially productive.

We've done this because, as with any Ponzi scheme, new growth provides the illusion of prosperity. In the near term, revenue grows, while the corresponding maintenance obligations -- which are not counted on the public balance sheet -- are a generation away.

In the late 1970s and early 1980s, we completed one life cycle of the suburban experiment, and at the same time, growth in America slowed. There were many reasons involved, but one significant factor was that our suburban cities were now starting to experience cash outflows for infrastructure maintenance. We'd reached the "long term," and the end of easy money.

It took us a while to work through what to do, but we ultimately decided to go "all in" using leverage. In the second life cycle of the suburban experiment, we financed new growth by borrowing staggering sums of money, both in the public and private sectors. By the time we crossed into the third life cycle and flamed out in the foreclosure crisis, our financing mechanisms had, out of necessity, become exotic, even predatory.

One of humanity's greatest strengths -- our ability to innovate solutions to complex problems -- can be a detriment when we misdiagnose the problem. Our problem was not, and is not, a lack of growth. Our problem is 60 years of unproductive growth -- growth that has buried us in financial liabilities. The American pattern of development does not create real wealth. It creates the illusion of wealth. Today we are in the process of seeing that illusion destroyed, and with it the prosperity we have come to take for granted.

That is now our greatest immediate challenge. We've actually embedded this experiment of suburbanization into our collective psyche as the "American dream," a non-negotiable way of life that must be maintained at all costs. What will we throw away trying to sustain the unsustainable? How much of our dwindling wealth will be poured into propping up this experiment gone awry?

We need to end our investments in the suburban pattern of development, along with the multitude of direct and indirect subsidies that make it all possible. Further, we need to intentionally return to our traditional pattern of development, one based on creating neighborhoods of value, scaled to actual people. When we do this, we will inevitably rediscover our traditional values of prudence and thrift as well as the value of community and place.

The way we achieve real, enduring prosperity is by building an America full of what I call Strong Towns.

FAITH AND COMMUNITY

(September 12, 2011) Six years ago I received a phone call from a group of Hasidic Jews from Brooklyn, NY. They asked if I would be interested in helping them build a city from scratch in rural Kansas. For a Catholic farm boy from rural Minnesota, this strange request became one of the most important opportunities of my life.

Not because I got to build the city. That would have been great, but the project fell apart before it even really got started, the logistics of relocating intact a community of Orthodox Jews halfway across the country too daunting for them (and perhaps me, too) to pull off. The opportunity came from how the experience changed my spiritual life and helped me understand the value of community.

I was brought up Catholic, but I don't want to pretend that my experience was normal or typical. It may be, but I understand now that faith and religion are what we make of it. I struggled many years to make it work for me, trying to adapt my life to the teachings I was receiving and trying to place those teachings into a context I could relate to. When given the choice, I quit the church, came back again, drifted away, came back.... I don't think this is abnormal for a young man.

Much of my periods of disillusionment and most of my periods of devotion centered around my own life. My faith was very much about me. If I did the right things and lived a good life, I would end up in heaven. Jesus died on the cross so I could have eternal life. I had, or attempted to have, a relationship with God, and that connection was between God and me. There were times I felt alone (like Army basic training) that this brought me great comfort, but many times when this relationship was daunting, overwhelming and -- ironically -- isolating. I tried very hard -- even seriously investigated whether I had a calling to the priesthood -- but ultimately felt like I failed at the effort more than I succeeded.

In 2000, I had the opportunity to visit Italy for six weeks. This would be my first trip abroad and I was excited to experience life in a largely Catholic society in the heart of Catholicism. I looked at it as an opportunity to walk amongst people who lived their faith as part of their community. The trip was fantastic, but it was anything but a deeply spiritual experience. I can sum it up with one example: Participating in mass at St. Peter's basilica in Vatican City, the Italian woman sitting in front of me took three separate calls on her cell phone, including one on her way to communion, and while my Italian was not great, it was clear none of these conversations were remotely critical. Religiously, I was disillusioned. Was a life of substance and faith simply not possible within a modern society?

What my eyes were not seeing, and what my English-only ears were not hearing, was the fabric of the community. Walking with a dear friend of mine through the streets of one small town in Southern Italy, I asked her why she -- a very smart, very accomplished but quite unappreciated Italian woman -- did not move to America where women are given more opportunity. She had lived in the United States for a year and, with that experience of my world, told me flatly that I did not understand *la dolce vita*, the sweet life she had there, surrounded by her family and friends.

The Hasidic helped me to understand this better. The ones I came to know live deliberately as a tight community in various Brooklyn neighborhoods. They dress alike. The men grow their beards. The women shave their heads. They have their own schools that emphasize the teaching of Hebrew texts. Their children don't typically mingle amongst the sexes. They speak Yiddish. They eat kosher foods and have cleansing rituals. The ones I met did not have television. They even have their own ambulance services as well as their own state-sanctioned court system.

All of this is very strange to the typical American. It is sometimes controversial too. A proposal to put a bike path through one of these deeply Hasidic neighborhoods was aggressively opposed by the Hasidic community. They did not want what in comparison to their conservative dress would be scantily clad people biking through their neighborhoods. I understand the bike advocates that were upset by the political clout the Hasidic voting block used to have the path moved. For a country that is supposed to be a melting pot, the way the Hasidic have clung together as a group can sometimes be hard to understand and a little bit threatening.

There are other parts of their life that are, however, incontrovertibly beautiful. My most endearing Hasidic friend -- his name is Moshe, also called Mark -- lived in 2005 in a very small apartment with his wife and three children. By small, I mean far smaller than the college apartment I shared with my brother. His living room also served as a dining room and, at night, a bedroom for the older children. These were tight quarters. Despite this, the family had taken in two young (and very cranky) infants during my time there. Why had they done this? I was told that the parents of these children were having a tough time and they were trying to help out. Did they know these parents? Not really, but they knew they needed help.

I saw example after example of this type of beautiful community awareness. We would walk along the street and, as if Mark was some type of Jewish Santa Claus, the kids would gather around and he'd stoop down and say hi to them. We'd cross the street and everyone would greet each other, most often by name. He'd tell me something about many of them -- their family history or relation to his. We'd dine with different collections of people; some engaged in our project, some working on a new school, some dealing with a social issue and some just to chat. The feeling of community in all its joy and sorrow, all its greatness and imperfection, was omnipresent.

It was this experience that started me on a transition where my Catholic faith went from one of a personal and rather self-serving relationship with God and into one of seeing the teachings of Jesus through the prism of community. Jesus was, after all, a teacher whose central message was how to live together, in communion with God, during the oppression of the domination system established by the Roman Empire.

Love thy neighbor. Do unto others as you would have them do unto you. If someone wants your tunic, hand him your cloak as well. Forgive us our debts, as we forgive our debtors. Do not notice the splinter in your neighbor's eye without acknowledging the beam in your own. The story of the good Samaritan. These are radical teachings for creating a just world that continue to resonate here and now in our own places.

No story captures this community-centric view more than the story of the feeding of five thousand. Growing up, this was a story of a miracle. I was taught that Jesus, a divine figure throughout his human life and thus possessing powers greater than any of us, turned five loaves and two fish into enough food to feed five thousand. What I took away from this is that Jesus had supreme power, but I never understood why -- especially in a time of brutal hunger and suffering like the first century AD -- he didn't just feed everyone. Here's the passage from Matthew, Chapter 14:

> *"and he ordered the crowds to sit down on the grass. Taking the five loaves and the two fish, and looking up to heaven, he said the blessing, broke the loaves, and gave them to the disciples, who in turn gave them to the crowds. They all ate and were satisfied, and they picked up the fragments left over--twelve wicker baskets full. Those who ate were about five thousand men, not counting women and children."*

What if this isn't a story about the exercise of divine power but something more applicable to you and me? What if this is a story about community? What if the message is: if we share what we have, there will be abundance for everyone? In antiquity's version of the modern children's story *Stone Soup*, we all give the little we have and the community prospers. This is not an un-American idea. These are actually the principles that every little town in our country was established around.

They are more real to me now than the faith of my childhood. I see it most in practice today when I am fortunate to spend time with my Hasidic friend. In the brief three hours we got to hang out together last Friday, we talked about his grandfather, a Holocaust survivor. Mark told me he felt bad about not going to visit him often enough, that he felt a strong obligation to care for him and some others that were not doing well in his community. *"I feel fortunate to be able to help them,"* he said. *"And God knows, I may need others to help me someday."*

Mark took me to the new World Trade Center, the site of Ground Zero and the 9/11 Memorial. It was two days before the 10-year anniversary and there was a lot going on. I reflected on that feeling I think we all had in the days after the attack, that one you would have liked to "bottle" and hold on to. It wasn't bipartisanship the way our crass politicians would have us believe. It was community. It was that notion, however fleeting, that the person next to you was your neighbor as Jesus would have defined "neighbor". It was the realization that we are connected, that we are all in this together. In the midst of such despair, it was a beautiful feeling that many of us remember vividly.

As I prepared to leave for the airport and my flight home, Mark and his family were preparing for the beginning of the Sabbath at sundown. I asked him what it meant to him, the weekly Sabbath. He picked up his Blackberry and held it for me to look at. *"All week I focus on this. I always have business or something going on. Always texting. Always working on something. At sundown it stops, and for just one day I shut it all off and focus on the things that are most important."*

Those things -- prayer, family and community -- could go a long ways towards helping us today.

ABOUT THE AUTHOR

Charles Marohn is a father, husband and an imaginer of great things. He is the founder of the Strong Towns movement and currently serves as Executive Director of Strong Towns, a 501(c)3 non-profit organization. He is an author, columnist, podcaster, amateur videographer and public speaker.

Marohn has a Bachelor's degree in Civil Engineering from the University of Minnesota's Institute of Technology. He is a licensed engineer in the state of Minnesota. He also has received a Master's of Urban and Regional Planning from the University of Minnesota's Humphrey Institute. He holds certification from the American Institute of Certified Planners.

Marohn is a member of the Congress for the New Urbanism and is active in their NextGen affiliation. He is also a member of the American Planning Association and the National Society of Professional Engineers.

Charles, his wife, their two daughters and their two Samoyeds live north of Brainerd, MN.

* * * * *

The best way to contact Charles Marohn is through the Strong Towns Network, a social media site he helped establish to share the technical side of strong towns concepts and to assist local officials and changemakers in implementing a strong towns approach. That effort is online at www.StrongTowns.net.

You can also reach him at:

Facebook: www.facebook.com/marohn

Twitter: www.twitter.com/clmarohn

LinkedIn: www.linkedin.com/in/charlesmarohn

ABOUT STRONG TOWNS

A 501(c)3 organization has been established to develop and promote the concept of a strong town. The mission of that organization is to support a model of growth that allows America's towns to become financially strong and resilient.

StrongTowns.org maintains the Strong Towns Blog, the Strong Towns Podcast and See it Differently (SID) tv, all popular channels for strong towns thought that together reach thousands each week. In 2010, Strong Towns published the Curbside Chat, a report on financial realities facing America's cities towns and neighborhoods. The free booklet is a companion guide to the Strong Towns presentation of the same name.

You can connect with Strong Towns on Facebook, Twitter, YouTube and iTunes.

ENDNOTES

ⁱ There is more depth to each of these case studies. The rural road is actually the road I currently live on. It was one of the earliest case studies I did, a back-of-the-envelope calculation I did when I received my annual property tax statement.

The suburban road was a messy project in the city of Afton, MN, where one of the most near-sighted city councils I have ever worked with essentially spent all the city's reserves fixing one minor road, the only apparent reason being that the residents on that road came to every council meeting. The decision was made after they received and discussed the memo wrote on it, so they were clearly aware of the implications.

The street serving the high value homes and the urban street in decline were both contained in larger studies I did for communities. The former project was never accepted by the city of Pequot Lakes, MN, the memo I put together being a primary factor in killing the project. For the latter, some tough decisions are yet to be made in the city of Perham, MN, where a hospital just built on the edge of town where all of the action seems to be shifting, quite distressingly.

The rural industrial park case study was included in a plan I wrote for the city of Walker, MN. That project has not proceeded although, to my amazement, they are still pursuing it despite a full understanding of the long term implications. (What else are we supposed to do, they say.)

The suburban industrial park project is also dead, largely due to the deeper understanding that the city of Pequot Lakes, MN, has developed over the last few years. I work closely with them serving as their city planner and have been successful in embedding Strong Towns thinking into the thought process of many there. Ironically, the original industrial park project was one that I worked on in my early days as an engineer.

The small town wastewater system in Backus, MN, is such a tragic project. When I originally wrote about it, the city was pursuing funding to fix their system. Due to financial incentives for communities that work cooperatively with their neighbors, they have now changed their plans and are trying to pump their sewage to the neighboring community, at much greater cost and, ultimately, making the city even less resilient than it is today.

Finally, the Tower Historic Harbor project, which is one of the most bizarre I have ever written about, is going ahead full steam. It will actually wind up to be the swan song project for U.S. Representative James Oberstar, the powerful congressman from Minnesota who chaired the House Transportation Committee before being defeated in 2010. While I don't question the Representative's intentions, I do believe that Minnesota's Arrowhead Region will ultimately curse him when the bill for maintaining all of the massive infrastructure he was able to get built starts to come due. Since all of the public money he secured for his district didn't provide anything more than the short term illusion of prosperity for this chronically poor region, the hangover is going to be extra cruel.

[ii] My joint hometowns of Brainerd and Baxter, MN, provide a unique laboratory to examine the impact of the Suburban Experiment on an historic railroad town (Brainerd) and pure auto-oriented development (Baxter). At the Strong Towns Blog this is an ongoing series that has revealed many insights.

[iii] For those wanting a quick overview of the Interstate Highway System, I've found the entry on Wikipedia to be a real good summary. http://en.wikipedia.org/wiki/Interstate_Highway_System

[iv] While I do not have a comprehensive and current list of state DOT's and their funding deficits, the narrative is familiar as I travel across the country. In my state of Minnesota, it is $2.5 billion per year. For California, it is $37 billion per year. For Pennsylvania, it is $3.5 billion per year. All of these numbers far exceed the annual spending of these departments. In an era of austerity, they don't just need a percentage increase in their budgets. To keep up, they need their budgets to double or more in size.

[v] While I myself tend to be an advocate of limited government, I've written and spoken out a number of times in opposition to my home state's most prominent politician, Michele Bachmann, whose support of the big government spending on the $668 million St. Croix bridge project in her district typifies the incoherence of her brand of conservatism.

[vi] Official cost/benefit analyses are a professional fraud I have written about a number of times, most prominently in 2010 when a Minnesota community was awarded a TIGER grant from the federal government. To give you a quick sense of the disingenuousness of this approach, these analyses are used primarily to convert small increments of saved travel time into enormous "economic" benefits in order to justify spending on projects, but this same rigor is never applied to "improvements" like new intersections or signals that impede traffic flow. Doing the latter would mean fewer projects would be built, a negative outcome for those working in the system.

[vii] *Initial Jobless Claims in U.S. Fell Last Week to 400,000,* Bloomberg News, August 4, 2011.

[viii] The American Society of Civil Engineers periodically issues a Report Card on America's Infrastructure, always giving the American systems a low mark and

calling for more money to be spent but failing to provide any context or alternative approaches.

ix When this essay originally ran on the Strong Towns Blog, I had linked to a number of news articles, political press releases and blogs that all parroted the ASCE line verbatim.

x As I write this, we are currently taxing at less than 20% of GDP, although many projections I have seen show this rate rising to over 20% GDP to meet the entitlement obligations of the country. My personal belief is that projections such as these are silly, especially in times of high volatility, so I've not spent a lot of time here trying to discern a consensus estimate.

xi Neal Peirce interviewed me for his article. I have never spoken with Ms. Caldwell or anyone at the American Society of Civil Engineers since my days as an undergraduate at the University of Minnesota.

xii The Curbside Chat is one of the primary public outreach and engagement initiatives at Strong Towns. You can learn more about the Curbside Chat or request that we hold one in your community by visiting www.CurbsideChat.org.

xiii Joe Minicozzi is a friend of mine and someone whose work I really admire. He is a dynamic thinker and speaker and, for a city struggling to find answers to financial and planning questions, there are few in his league that you can turn to. As of this writing, you can reach Minicozzi through his professional practice at www.urban-three.com.

xiv Right now my home school district, ISD 181 in Minnesota, has established busing zones that begin one mile from the school. If the inequalities and perverse incentives are overwhelming. ISD 181, like so many others, picks up the children of wealthy families that live outside of town, providing them door-to-door service, while the children of the poor families that live in town are forced to walk to school. The fact that we take money out of the classroom and increase class sizes to do this is even more depressing.

xv The precise regulation requiring school districts to provide free busing to students is Minnesota Administrative Rule 3520.1500.

xvi I obtained the transportation budget numbers from the District's website.

xvii I obtained the average salary information from the District's website.

xviii The source for this chart is the website Econbrowser.

xix This quote is from a Reuter's article published March 22, 2011, titled *Portugal government may collapse before EU summit.*

[xx] This quote is from a NY Times article published March 22, 2011, titled *Austerity Triggers Portugal Standoff.*

[xxi] This quote is from a CNBC article published March 22, 2011, titled *US Approaching Insolvency, Fix To Be 'Painful': Fisher.*

[xxii] The deficit projection for 2010 from the Office of Management and Budget was $970 billion while the actual deficit was $1.6 trillion.

[xxiii] More on the Mechanisms of Growth is available from the Strong Towns website.

[xxiv] I've used this project a number of times in speeches and writings because it is a great example. For the record, the city I'm referring to is Remer, MN, and the project would be the wastewater improvements that happened there around 2001.

[xxv] The Republican caucus in Minnesota had a large number of rural legislators, while the Democratic Farm Labor caucus contained a large contingency from the urban areas of Minneapolis and St. Paul. Since local government aid in Minnesota goes predominantly to small towns and large cities (not suburbs), Republican proposals to reduce local government aid conveniently exempted small towns. Strong Towns issued a report on the impact of local government aid on our cities, which can be found at www.StrongTowns.org.

[xxvi] The Strong Towns website, www.StrongTowns.org, contains a complete list of Strong Towns Placemaking Principles.

[xxvii] These statistics come from a July 31, 2011, report in the International Business Times titled *US Economy: Weaker Than Thought.*

[xxviii] This data came from a July 31, 2011, press release from the Bureau of Economic Analysis of the Department of Commerce.

[xxix] This quote came from an online article in the Minneapolis Star Tribune. The paper removes articles from public access after a certain time period and I was not able to verify the date of publication or provide a link.

[xxx] Incidentally, I was interviewed for the series but nothing I said was used or apparently influenced the article in any way. I did not validate the reporter's thesis – or contradict it in a way that disputed his thesis -- but there were many people quoted within who did. I found the entire thing a silly distraction, like arguing over the best way to commit suicide. Is there really a "best" way? If your story is about one of the two options, you really won't be interested in the existential question.

[xxxi] I'd recommend the book Superfreakonomics because it is really fun and

entertaining.

xxxii These statistics were obtained from the National Center for Health Statistics.

xxxiii I was criticized by more than one person for using the 9/11 reference, as if I were being gratuitous. I mean no offense to those directly or indirectly impacted by 9/11 (I would certainly be in at least the latter of those groups) but I do find it compelling to make the comparison because they are equally horrific (some may argue that the number of child deaths is even more horrific), yet our reaction to the attrition levels of driving borders on acceptance where our collective outrage by 9/11 has been anything but. I am not calling for less outrage over the terrorist attacks but more awareness of the dangers of driving.

xxxiv When I started looking into this, it was actually quite appalling. Not a single agency or advocacy organization that dealt with child safety that I came across ever recommended, or even suggested, that the safest thing for a child is to limit the amount of time they are on the road. The message was clearly, "just put them in a car seat."

xxxv Federal Reserve Chairman Ben Bernanke made this statement on July 13, 2011, in testimony before the U.S. House Financial Services Committee.

xxxvi This quote appeared in the online publication GoLocal Prov on September 2, 2011.

xxxvii This information came from the Courage to Connect website.

xxxviii This book review appeared in the Wall Street Journal on April 22, 2011, and was titled *Where the Action Is*.

xxxix Steve Mouzon's work can be found online at www.originalgreen.org.

xl The discussions of the Incremental Sprawl Repair group can be found online at isrworkinggroup.posterous.com.

xli More on Galina Tachieva and her work is available at www.sprawlrepair.com.

xlii For some short background information on Celebration, Wikipedia is a good source.

xliii More information on the SmartCode is available at Smart Code Central.

xliv You can follow Nate Hood on Twitter at @Nathaniel1983.

[xlv] A July 2, 2012 article in the Kansas City Star titled, *Federal highway fund is running on fumes*, gives a good overview of how the fund is broke and how there are no coherent or viable plans to bring it back to solvency.

[xlvi] This quote is from an August 16, 2011, article on the website Chron.com titled *Perry's Texas: Transportation needs left unmet.*

[xlvii] In 2010 I wrote a long series on cost/benefit analyses. You can find it with a Google search for "Strong Towns Best of Blog Cost Benefit".

[xlviii] This statistic comes from data provided by an organization called Redfields to Greenfields.

[xlix] I did a TEDx talk on this topic, which you may enjoy. It is available on YouTube.com and is called *The Important Difference Between a Road and a Street.*

[l] This definition can be found in the Missouri Statutes, Section 300.010.

[li] This quote is from a website on the history of the diverging diamond, www.divergingdiamond.com/history.html.

[lii] This quote comes from a January 28, 2010 article in USA Today titled, *Missouri test drives 'diverging diamond' interchange.*

[liii] This quote is taken from the Fresh Energy website.

[liv] If you would like more information on how these calculations are done, you can read my 2010 essays on Costs and Benefits. You can find them with a Google search for "Strong Towns Best of Blog Cost Benefit".

[lv] More on the *Mechanisms of Growth* is available from the Strong Towns website.

[lvi] The ASCE Report Card on America's Infrastructure is available at www.infrastructurereportcard.org.

Made in the USA
Charleston, SC
26 November 2013